W9-BKZ-277

How to Cook *Everything*™

Holiday Cooking

Other Books by Mark Bittman:

How to Cook Everything™

How to Cook Everything™: Quick Cooking

How to Cook Everything™: Vegetarian Cooking

How to Cook Everything™: Easy Weekend Cooking

How to Cook Everything™: The Basics

The Minimalist Cooks at Home

The Minimalist Cooks Dinner

The Minimalist Entertains

Fish: The Complete Guide to Buying and Cooking

Leafy Greens

With Jean-Georges Vongerichten:

Simple to Spectacular

Jean-Georges: Cooking at Home with a Four-Star Chef

How to Cook *Everything*™

Holiday Cooking

Mark Bittman

Illustrations by Alan Witschonke

WILEY

Wiley Publishing, Inc.

Published by Wiley Publishing, Inc., Hoboken, NJ

For general information on our other products and services or to obtain technical support please contact our Customer Care Department within the U.S. at 800-762-2974, outside the U.S. at 317-572-3993 or fax 317-572-4002.

Wiley also publishes its books in a variety of electronic formats. Some content that appears in print may not be available in electronic books.

Library of Congress Cataloging-in-Publication Data:

Bittman, Mark.
 How to cook everything. Holiday cooking / Mark Bittman ; illustrations by Alan Witschonke.
  p. cm.
 ISBN 0-7645-2512-3 (Paperback : alk. paper)
 1. Holiday cookery. 2. Menus. I. Title.
 TX739.B52 2003
 641.5'68—dc21

                    2003008739

Manufactured in the United States of America

10 9 8 7 6 5 4 3 2 1

Photos on pages 40, 50, and 82 © PhotoDisc, Inc. / Getty Images
Photos on pages xii, 12, 26, 64, and 102 by David Bishop

To my parents and my kids

WILEY PUBLISHING, INC.

Publisher: Natalie Chapman

Executive Editor: Anne Ficklen

Senior Editor: Linda Ingroia

Production Editor: Heather Wilcox

Cover Design: Cecelia Diskin

Interior Design: Edwin Kuo and Anthony Bagliani, Solid Design

Interior Layout: Holly Wittenberg

Manufacturing Buyer: Kevin Watt

Contents

Acknowledgments

I have been writing about food for nearly 25 years, and it's impossible to thank all the people who have helped me make a go of it during that time. Most of them know who they are—we have shared cooking, eating, and talking, much of what constitutes my life—and together I do owe them a broad "thanks."

However, some special friends and colleagues have been there for me and helped me out in recent years, and I want to thank them especially: Mitchell Orfuss, Naomi Glauberman, John Bancroft, Madeline Meacham, David Paskin, Pamela Hort, Jack Hitt, Semeon Tsalbins, Susan Moldow, Bill Shinker, Jim Nelson, Fred Zolna, Sherry Slade, Lisa Sanders, Genevieve Ko, Charlie Pinsky, Geof Drummond, Sam Sifton, Nancy Cobb, and Steve Rubin.

I have been blessed, too, with great colleagues at Wiley: Linda Ingroia, who has worked tirelessly on the new *How to Cook Everything*™ series; Edwin Kuo, Jeffrey Faust, Cecelia Diskin, and Holly Wittenberg for great covers and interiors; Heather Wilcox, the production editor, and Christina Van Camp for keeping keen eyes on clarity and consistency; and Kate Fischer and Michelle Sewell for managing *How to Cook Everything* publicity opportunities. Jennifer Feldman got the *How to Cook Everything* series up and running, and Natalie Chapman and Robert Garber have given it tremendous support. My agent, Angela Miller, is simply the best, and has been a terrific influence in my life for over a decade; huge thanks to her, as always.

Few of my cookbooks would have been written without the help and inspiration of Karen Baar, to whom I remain grateful. And, as always, special thanks to my fabulous children, Kate and Emma, and my most frequent companions, John H. Willoughby, John Ringwald, and Alisa X. Smith, all of whom give me invaluable love and perspective on a daily basis, and newfound confidence in the world of cooking.

How to Cook Everything: Holiday Cooking is an easy-to-use collection of my favorite recipes for the biggest special occasions and parties of the year. There's an emphasis on food for the major autumn holidays: Thanksgiving, Christmas, Hanukkah, and New Year's Eve; it addresses the feasts, family time, entertaining—and, let's get this clear, stress—that goes on during these months. Many people cook more often and with greater relish in the late fall to early winter, and this collection reflects that. Of course, you can use this book to also plan meals for Valentine's Day, Easter, Passover, Mother's Day, Father's Day, Independence Day, or any other day of the year.

There is no doubt that cooking for a holiday can be stressful; even if you love cooking, there's a greater demand on your time, energy, budget, organizational skills, and knowledge. The idea here is to offer good recipes and sound overall techniques and strategies—in short, guidance—to get you through it. This book not only will help you to prepare holiday feasts, but also to cook for casual and formal sit-down dinners and for party buffets. The recipes can usually be varied to your taste or diet, or what's available in your kitchen, so consider this book a potential guide for specific meals, but more important, it is a springboard for your own creativity.

In addition to more than 90 recipes, like the classics Roast Turkey and Gravy, Baked Ham with Maple Glaze, and Pecan Pie, there are recipes newer to the American kitchen, as well as party foods like Potato Pancakes (latkes); Seafood Salad, Adriatic-Style; and Chocolate Truffles. I've also included dozens of variations; tips to help you shop for, prepare, and cook the recipes; lists of flavoring ideas; and illustrations on some tricky techniques like shucking clams and carving turkey.

If you're interested, and if it will help you plan your meals, many of the recipes should or can be made in advance, so you're not juggling the work of cooking five dishes right before you need to serve them. (You should enjoy your own gatherings, too.) These recipes are labeled with a 🅜 icon.

If you're looking for holiday meal ideas, go to the menu pages (112–115) in the back. You'll find 25 menus for traditional meals, plus ideas for the holiday season, such as a Shopping Night Dinner, casual Holiday Dinner with Friends, and Holiday Gifts from the Kitchen.

When it comes to holiday cooking, I imagine your goals and mine are the same—to make good food for celebrations and gatherings of family and friends, without dedicating crazy amounts of time and effort to it. This book can help you do that.

What to Know About Holiday Cooking

Cooking for a holiday can be enormously gratifying. Particularly for the big holidays in the fall, starting in November, even those people who don't cook much during the year begin to spend a considerable amount of time envisioning, planning and shopping, and creating parties and special meals for Thanksgiving, Christmas, Hanukkah, New Year's Eve, Kwanzaa, Three Kings Day, and the rest of the mosaic of winter feasts that comprise the holiday season. And during the holiday season we all tend to entertain more, so you're also thinking about party foods—whether for sit-down dinners or party buffets. During the spring and summer, it's also fun to entertain for special occasions, but even "simple" outdoor meals require planning and appropriate recipes.

Presumably, this is all a labor of love. But there is no denying that all of this planning and cooking is time-consuming and, ultimately, extremely anxiety-inducing.

What will get you through the holidays with your good spirit intact is the same as what works for home cooks during the rest of the year (but at the holidays has to be done with more focus and forethought): Keep your pantry well stocked; plan ahead; get others to help out with the shopping, preparation, cooking, and cleanup; and, most important, plan according to your abilities and your needs. Do not be overly ambitious: A six-course Thanksgiving meal at which everyone is happy is far better, regardless of the food, than a twelve-course meal at which the host has a nervous breakdown. We've all seen this. If one true purpose of the holidays is to share meals with people you care about, there is every reason to pay attention to quality but very little to impress anyone with quantity.

Cooking Basics

Here are some thoughts and guidelines on efficient, safe, and smart cooking in general and on cooking at holiday time in particular.

Time

Time is always precious, but during the holidays, you've got more demands on your time, especially if you want to host holiday meals at your house or you like to entertain. There are no better ways to show your love than preparing high-quality food, so this is time well spent.

It's easy to have the makings of a meal or two on hand at all times just by maintaining the right mix of staples—even if friends invite themselves over at the last minute and suddenly become hungry.

Different people like to eat different ways, obviously, but certain foods belong in every kitchen all the time, and keep nearly indefinitely.

To stock your pantry and refrigerator, make sure you have on hand:

- pasta and other grains, especially rice
- canned beans and other vegetables, especially tomatoes
- spices, and dried herbs when fresh are unavailable
- jarred olives, anchovies, and capers
- liquid seasonings such as olive oil (extra-virgin), vinegar (sherry, balsamic, high-quality red or white wine), and soy sauce
- flour, cornmeal, and the like

- nuts and dried fruits
- onions, potatoes, garlic, and other long-keeping vegetables
- non-fat dried milk (usually for emergencies)
- canned or boxed broth such as chicken, beef, and vegetable
- baking staples such as baking powder, vanilla extract, baking chocolate, canned pumpkin, and so on
- eggs and butter

With this list alone you will be equipped to make literally dozens of different dishes, from salads to sweets. When you throw in the fresh ingredients that you're likely to have in the refrigerator as a result of special shopping jaunts—vegetables, herbs, fruit, meat, fish, milk, cream, cheese, and other perishables—the result is that you'll be able to prepare most of the 90 recipes in this book without going out to search for special ingredients.

In general, I consider whole, fresh ingredients a priority. Of course, when time is an issue, I am not against the use of store-bought broth, or frozen spinach, as part of a recipe, especially where the ordinary-at-best nature of such products is disguised by the other ingredients in the recipe. But I do not believe in "miracle" recipes based on canned or dried soups, artificial mayonnaise, or powdered desserts. Real cakes begin with flour and butter, and real whipped cream does not come from a can. This is a cookbook, not a chemistry class; to cook good dishes you must start with real food.

This book can be your guide for those classic and special recipes worth repeating for every holiday as well as a source for inventive variations. It's fun to consider each holiday a new beginning or a creative challenge, making it more of a pleasure than a chore, but it's practically impossible to plan a new menu for each holiday; as you know, new recipes take more work than those with which you are already familiar. So keep those traditions in your plan—the roast turkey you know well, your aunt's best dessert—and vary some of the other dishes, including the ones you don't know well.

A word about recipe timing. The timing for every recipe is always approximate. The rate at which food cooks is dependent on the moisture content and temperature of the food itself; measurements (which are rarely perfectly accurate); heat level (everyone's "medium-high" heat is not the same, and most ovens are off by at least 25°F in one direction or another); the kind of equipment (some pans conduct heat better than others); even the air temperature. So be sure to use time as a rough guideline, AND judge doneness by touch, sight, and taste.

Food Safety

When you are doing a lot more cooking for the holidays and are pressed for time you may easily slip into shortcuts that could compromise your food safety. Most food-borne illnesses can be prevented, so it's worth taking precautions.

Keep your hands and all food preparation surfaces and utensils perfectly clean—soap and hot water are all you need. Wash cutting boards after using, and don't prepare food directly on your counters unless you wash them as well. Change sponges frequently, too, and throw your sponges in the washing machine whenever you wash clothes in hot water. (Or microwave your sponge every day.) Change your kitchen towel frequently, also—at least once a day.

It should go without saying that your refrigerator functions well (35°F is about right) and food should be stored in the refrigerator until just before cooking or whenever you're not using it. Your freezer should be at 0°F or lower. Thaw foods in the refrigerator, or under cold running water. And never place cooked food on a plate that previously held raw food.

Those are the easy parts, which everyone should do without question. The other parts—cooking foods to a safe temperature—are more difficult. Of common foods, cooked vegetables and grains are the safest; next comes cooked fish; then comes cooked meat other than hamburger; then comes cooked chicken, eggs, and hamburger, with which most concerns are associated. I don't advocate cooking all meats until they are well done (and inedible), but work with the tastes and doneness that you're comfortable with. I cook turkey to 165°F (measured, with an instant-read thermometer, in a couple of places in the thigh); this is lower than the USDA recommendations, but if the thermometer is accurate it's safe, and the bird is not hideously overcooked.

My overall strategy is that I keep a spotlessly clean kitchen, wash my hands about 40 times a day, and cook food so that it tastes as good as it can—that's how the recipes in this book are designed.

Equipment

Every kitchen should have basic equipment (described fully in *How to Cook Everything*), but some things are more essential at holiday time than others. These include:

Food processor: Practically a necessity for large-scale cooking.

Electric mixer: If you bake a lot, you will want both a powerful standing mixer and a small, handheld mixer. If you bake occasionally, you will want either.

Blender (upright and/or handheld): For drinks and soups.

Stockpot: Ultimately, the leftovers go here.

Large roasting pan: Like a lasagne pan, sturdy, with two handles and (preferably) a nonstick surface.

Grill and grill tools: Grills are major appliances, so I'd say adding one is like adding an oven…

Pie plates: You will probably need more than one; 9 inches is standard.

Loaf pans: If you're going to bake bread.

Muffin tins: If people are staying for breakfast.

Carving knife: Not something you will use every day, but really handy for large birds and roasts.

Instant-read thermometer: The most accurate way to determine whether food is done, especially for inexperienced cooks. You may never have cooked a turkey in your life, but when that thermometer reads 165°F, you know it's done.

Rolling pin: Try making a pie crust without one. Buy a straight rolling pin without ball bearings; it's lighter, more easily maneuvered, and unbreakable.

Zester: The easiest way to remove zest from lemons and other citrus (but not the only way; you can remove zest with a vegetable peeler and mince it by hand).

1 | Hors D'Oeuvres

Ⓜ Make Ahead

Roasted Buttered Nuts

Simple as these are, they are a revelation, so far from canned mixed nuts that you may have trouble believing it. For one thing, canned mixed nuts are almost always heavy on peanuts and Brazil nuts, both of which are inexpensive. But the first are common, and the second become rancid very quickly after being shelled. For your own mix, I suggest relying heavily on pecans, almonds, and cashews, with a sprinkling of anything else you can lay your hands on, from hazelnuts (filberts) to pistachios to sunflower seeds.

Given that winter weather tends to be quite dry, you can make these several days ahead and they will remain crisp, even out in the open.

Makes 4 to 6 servings

Time: 15 minutes

---

2 cups (about 1 pound) unsalted mixed shelled nuts

1 tablespoon peanut oil or melted butter

Salt and freshly ground black pepper to taste

1 Preheat the oven to 450°F.

2 Toss the nuts in a bowl with the oil or butter, salt, and pepper. Place on a baking sheet and roast, shaking occasionally, until lightly browned, about 10 minutes. Cool before serving; they will crisp as they cool.

 Sautéed Buttered Nuts With more fat, even better tasting. Place 4 tablespoons (1/2 stick) butter or peanut oil in a large skillet and turn the heat to medium-low. When the butter melts or the oil is hot, add the nuts and cook, stirring, until lightly browned, about 10 minutes. Be patient; high heat will burn the nuts. As they cook, season with salt and pepper. Cool before serving.

 Spiced Buttered Nuts Add 1 teaspoon to 1 tablespoon of any spice mixture, such as chili powder or curry powder, to the mix. When roasting, toss the spice with the nuts at the beginning. When sautéing, add it to the butter or oil as it heats.

Marinated Olives

Olives are so much better when marinated than when eaten straight from the jar or barrel that most people assume there is some trick to them. But there is not, other than to start with good olives. I do not use red pepper flakes when I marinate olives, but many people like a little bit of heat here—the choice is yours.

Note that these keep, and improve in flavor, for several weeks in the refrigerator. Always bring to room temperature before serving.

Makes 10 servings or more

Time: 5 minutes, plus marinating time

---

1 pound green or black olives, or a mixture, preferably imported from Greece, Italy, or Spain

1 teaspoon wine vinegar, or to taste

¼ cup extra-virgin olive oil

4 cloves garlic, crushed

Several sprigs fresh thyme, 1 teaspoon fresh thyme leaves, or ½ teaspoon dried thyme

2 bay leaves

1 teaspoon crushed red pepper flakes (optional)

1 Using the side of a broad knife, crush the olives lightly.

2 Mix together all other ingredients, mix in the olives, then pack into a jar or place in a serving bowl; taste, and add more vinegar if necessary. You can serve these immediately, although they are better if they sit, covered and refrigerated, for a day or two. Bring to room temperature before serving.

Ⓜ Marinated Olives with Lemon Add the minced zest of a lemon (a zester, which produces lovely strands, is the perfect tool for this) to the olives before marinating. Just before serving, toss in a few segments of lemon—cut the lemon in half through its equator and segment as you would a grapefruit.

Minced Vegetable Dip

The most basic of dips, and one you can almost always make with ingredients you have on hand. Feel free to substitute other vegetables if you don't have this exact combination. Make up to a couple of hours ahead, but don't toss veggies and dressing together until the last minute.

Makes at least 10 servings

Time: 10 minutes

---

1 cucumber

1 red bell pepper

1 scallion

1 cup sour cream or plain yogurt

1 tablespoon freshly minced dill leaves or 1 teaspoon dried dill

Salt and freshly ground black pepper to taste

Freshly squeezed lemon juice to taste (optional)

1 Peel the cucumber, then cut it in half the long way and scoop out the seeds. Stem and seed the pepper (you can peel this, too, if you like). Trim the scallion. If you're using yogurt, drain it for a few minutes in a cheesecloth-lined strainer.

2 Mince all the vegetables finely, or put them in the container of a food processor and pulse a few times; do not overprocess. You want to mince the vegetables, not puree them.

3 Mix the vegetables with the dill, sour cream, salt, and pepper; taste and adjust seasoning, adding a little lemon juice if necessary. Cover and refrigerate until ready to use. Serve with vegetables or crackers.

Real Onion Dip Omit the vegetables and dill. Add 1/2 cup very finely minced or pureed onion and 1/4 cup minced fresh parsley leaves.

Smoked Salmon or Trout Dip Omit the dill; omit or include the vegetables as you like. Add 1/2 cup flaked smoked trout or minced smoked salmon and 2 tablespoons minced fresh parsley leaves and lemon juice.

 # Hummus

Too often, hummus, which can be used as a dip or a spread, tastes like nothing but raw garlic; this is smoother and more complex in flavor. When making the chickpeas, let them cook a little longer than usual, so that they're nice and soft. (This is a good place to use canned chickpeas.)

Hummus may be made well in advance of serving, even a few days; but you run the risk that someone will find it in the refrigerator and eat it.

Makes at least 8 servings

Time: 20 minutes with precooked chickpeas

---

2 cups drained well-cooked or canned chickpeas

½ cup tahini (sesame paste)

¼ cup sesame oil from the top of the tahini or olive oil

1 small clove garlic, peeled, or to taste; or 1 tablespoon mashed Roasted Garlic (at right), plus more as needed

Salt and freshly ground black pepper to taste

1 tablespoon ground cumin, or to taste, plus a sprinkling for garnish

Juice of 1 lemon, plus more as needed

About ⅓ cup water, or as needed

1 teaspoon olive oil, approximately

1 Place everything except water and 1 teaspoon olive oil in the container of a food processor and begin to process; add water as needed to make a smooth puree.

2 Taste and add more garlic, salt, lemon juice, or cumin as needed. Serve, drizzled with a little olive oil and sprinkled with a bit of cumin. Serve with vegetables, crackers, or pita.

Ⓜ Roasted Garlic

Makes 2 heads • Time: About 1 hour

Roasted or simmered garlic is a wonderful condiment for bread or salads, and a great ingredient for any dish in which you want to add a lovely, mellow, but distinctively garlicky flavor.

You can cover and store the garlic, with the oil, in the refrigerator for a few days before using.

2 whole heads garlic	Salt
¼ cup water	1 tablespoon extra-virgin olive oil

1 Heat the oven to 375°F. Without breaking the heads apart, remove as much of the papery coating from them as you can.

2 Place the garlic and water in a small baking dish; sprinkle with salt and drizzle with the olive oil. Cover with aluminum foil and bake, basting with the oil-and-water mixture after about 30 minutes. Bake until the garlic is soft (you'll be able to pierce it easily with a thin-bladed knife), about 1 hour total.

Ⓜ **Faster Roasted Garlic** Break the heads into individual cloves, but do not peel them. Spread them on a baking sheet, sprinkle with salt, and drizzle with oil. Bake, shaking the pan occasionally, until tender, about 30 minutes.

Use this as a spread or a dip; its consistency is somewhere in between. Fresh goat cheese is just a little thicker than cottage cheese. This can be made a few hours in advance; don't add the olive oil until just before serving.

Makes at least 8 servings

Time: 10 minutes

1 pound fresh goat cheese

About 2 tablespoons cream, sour cream, plain yogurt, or milk

¼ teaspoon finely minced garlic, or to taste

½ cup mixed chopped fresh mild herbs, such as basil, parsley, chervil, dill, and/or chives

1 teaspoon minced fresh tarragon or ¼ teaspoon dried tarragon

Salt and freshly ground black pepper to taste

1 tablespoon extra-virgin olive oil

1 Thin the goat cheese with enough of the cream, sour cream, yogurt, or milk to give it a spreadable consistency; the amount will depend on the thickness of the cheese and whether you want a thick spread or a thinner dip.

2 Stir in the garlic and herbs. Taste and add salt if necessary (some goat cheese is quite salty) and pepper to taste. Drizzle with the olive oil and serve.

 Goat Cheese–Stuffed Figs This makes 4 to 8 servings. Take 8 ripe fresh figs and cut them in half. Use only ½ pound of goat cheese. Thin the cheese as above, just until it is thin enough to spread, but omit the garlic and herbs; taste the mixture and add salt if necessary. Spread about 1 tablespoon of the cheese onto the top of each fig, pressing just enough so that it adheres. Drizzle with a little olive oil, sprinkle with some freshly ground black pepper, and serve, or refrigerate for up to an hour, before garnishing and serving.

Simplest Cheese Straws

Easy, light, and quite irresistible. Consider adding fresh or dried herbs to the mix, and use any cheese you like, as long as it is hard enough to grate. Store, in a covered tin, for up to a few days before serving.

Makes 5 to 10 servings

Time: 20 minutes

---

1 pound cheddar or other hard, flavorful cheese

2 cups (about 9 ounces) all-purpose flour

Pinch cayenne

8 tablespoons (1 stick) chilled butter, plus a little more for greasing the baking sheet

Few drops ice water, if necessary

Coarse salt (optional)

1 Preheat the oven to 450°F.

2 Grate the cheese (you can use the food processor for this), then remove the cheese from the bowl. Add the flour and cayenne to the bowl and pulse. Cut the 8 tablespoons butter into pieces, then toss it in. Process until butter and flour are combined.

3 Remove the dough from the bowl and stir in the cheese. Knead by hand until it comes together, adding a few drops of ice water (no more than 1 tablespoon) if necessary. (You may prepare the recipe in advance up to this point; wrap well in plastic and refrigerate for up to 2 days before proceeding.)

4 Roll out into a rectangle about ¼ inch thick, then cut into strips as long as you like and about ½ inch wide. Place on a lightly greased baking sheet and sprinkle with the optional salt. Bake until golden brown, 5 to 8 minutes. Serve hot, warm, or at room temperature.

Marinated Mozzarella

If you can find small "mozzarella balls"—called *bocconcini*—by all means use them. Otherwise, cut a chunk of mozzarella into bite-sized pieces. In either case, use fresh mozzarella—which has the best flavor—if at all possible. You can marinate the cheese a day or so before serving it.

Makes 8 servings

Time: 20 minutes, plus resting time

¼ cup extra-virgin olive oil

¼ cup chopped fresh basil, parsley, or oregano leaves, or any combination

1 pound mozzarella (drained if packed in water), cut into bite-sized pieces if necessary

Salt and freshly ground black pepper to taste

Crushed red pepper flakes to taste

1 Combine the oil and the herb; toss in a bowl with the mozzarella.

2 Taste and add salt and the two peppers to taste. If possible, let stand for at least 30 minutes before serving.

Shopping Tip: In recent years, fresh mozzarella has begun to appear in more and more markets. Packed in water and sold in bulk, it is creamier, more tender, and more flavorful than the standard mozzarella sold dry and wrapped in plastic. Store it at home in its water and use it as quickly as possible, preferably within a day or two.

Bruschetta

Bruschetta is grilled (or broiled, or even toasted) bread, rubbed with garlic and drizzled with olive oil. There are two requirements: good coarse, crusty bread and good olive oil. Once you make basic bruschetta, you'll probably want to try variations; I give some, but the possibilities—as with any sandwich—are endless.

Makes 4 appetizer servings

Time: 20 minutes, plus time to preheat the grill

---

4 slices good bread, preferably cut from a large round loaf

Extra-virgin olive oil

1 clove garlic, halved

Salt to taste

1 Preheat the broiler or grill and adjust the rack so that it is at least 4 inches from the heat source. Brush the bread on one or both sides with a little olive oil and rub one or both sides of each slice with the garlic. (The energy you put into this will determine the intensity of the flavor of the finished product: Rub hard, letting the garlic disintegrate into the bread, and the flavor will be more pronounced; give it a cursory run-through, and the flavor will be mild.) Sprinkle with a little salt.

2 Broil or grill the bread until lightly browned on both sides, taking care not to burn it or toast it all the way through. If you like, drizzle with a little more olive oil and rub with more garlic. Serve immediately.

Bruschetta with Roasted or Simmered Garlic Prepare the bread with olive oil as above and broil or grill one side. Turn it over and broil or grill it for a minute or two longer on the other side. Spread the top with a tablespoon or so of mashed garlic puree (use Roasted Garlic, page 5, if you like); sprinkle with additional olive oil and salt if you like. Broil or grill until hot and lightly browned on top (broiler) or bottom (grill), taking care not to burn.

Bruschetta with Tomatoes and Basil Take care not to use overly juicy tomatoes or the bread will become soggy. (For this reason plum tomatoes are best.) Peel, core, seed, and dice 1 small-to-medium tomato per slice of bread. Drain in a strainer for a few minutes, while you preheat the grill or broiler. Prepare the bread with olive oil and garlic as above and broil or grill one side. Turn it over and broil or grill it for 1 minute on the other side, until hot and lightly brown, taking care not to burn. Spread the top with the tomato, then drizzle with olive oil. Garnish with torn or whole basil leaves (or other fresh herb), then drizzle with a little more olive oil and salt if you like.

A quiche is a savory open-faced pie, made with an unsweetened pie crust and usually served as part of a meal. It can be prepared up to a day ahead of time and reheated at the last moment or served at room temperature.

Makes 4 to 8 servings

Time: About 1½ hours

1 recipe Generous Pie Shell (from Flaky Pie Crust, page 88), made without sugar, in a 10-inch tart pan or 9-inch deep-dish pie pan, and chilled

6 eggs, at room temperature

2 cups grated Emmentaler, Gruyère, Cantal, cheddar, or other flavorful cheese

2 cups cream, half-and-half, or milk, gently heated just until warm

½ teaspoon salt

¼ teaspoon cayenne

1 Preheat the oven to 425°F. Prick the crust all over with a fork. Line it with tin foil and weight the bottom with a pile of dried beans, rice (these can be reused for this same purpose), or other weights that will sit flat on the surface. Bake 12 minutes. Remove from the oven and carefully remove the weight and foil; turn the oven to 325°F. Combine eggs, cheese, liquid, and seasonings; beat until blended.

2 Place the baked crust on a baking sheet. Pour the egg mixture into the crust, right to the top. Carefully transfer the baking sheet to the oven and bake 30 to 40 minutes, until the mixture is set but is still moist; it should still jiggle just a little in the middle. Cool on a rack and serve warm or at room temperature.

Preparation Tips: The doughs for quiches are best made with butter, but can also be made with olive oil. The flavor will be excellent, the texture not so great, but if you are off butter, you'll probably think the trade-off worthwhile.

Bear in mind that these are savory crusts, and so can be flavored in any way you like: Add 1 teaspoon of minced Roasted Garlic (page 5) to the crust, or 1 teaspoon to 1 tablespoon of any herb that you're using in the filling, for example. Cornmeal substituted for about one-quarter of the flour also makes for a nice change, adding crunch and flavor.

Cooking Tip: Like any custard, the filling should be cooked gently so it becomes creamy rather than hard. For this reason, and to keep the crusts crisp, crusts are precooked, then filled and returned to the oven at lower temperature.

 Bacon and Onion Quiche Step 1 is the same. While the crust is baking, cook 6 to 10 slices of good bacon in its own fat until nice and crisp. Remove the bacon with a slotted spoon and cook 6 cups thinly sliced onions in the bacon fat, stirring until very tender, at least 15 minutes. Mix with the eggs and the cream (omit the cheese). Place the bacon in the crust, pour the egg-onion mixture over it, and bake as in Step 2.

Ⓜ Spicy Chicken Kebabs

Here is a recipe that's great for parties year-round. It will work beautifully with any medium-dark meat, not only chicken thighs, but cubed turkey thighs, pork, and even sturdy fish such as swordfish or salmon.

Makes 4 servings

Time: About 1 hour, plus marinating time if you have it and time to preheat the grill

---

1 to 1½ pounds boneless chicken thighs, rinsed and patted dry with paper towels

Minced zest and juice of 1 lime

1 tablespoon peanut oil or other oil

1 tablespoon soy sauce

2 tablespoons minced garlic

2 tablespoons minced cilantro leaves, plus a bit more for garnish

¼ teaspoon cayenne, or to taste

2 tablespoons natural peanut butter

Salt and lots of freshly ground black pepper to taste

1 Cut the chicken thighs into 1- to 1½-inch cubes. Mix it together with all other ingredients and marinate, if you have the time, in a large dish or bowl in your refrigerator for 1 to 24 hours.

2 Start a charcoal or wood fire, or preheat a gas grill or broiler; the fire should be moderately hot. Remove the chicken from the marinade and boil the marinade for 1 minute. Thread the meat onto skewers and grill or broil about 4 inches from the heat source, basting with the sauce and turning every 2 or 3 minutes, until browned all over and cooked through (remove a piece and cut it in half to check), a total of 8 to 12 minutes. Garnish with cilantro leaves and serve.

Preparation Tip: If you plan to use wooden skewers for grilling, soak them first in cold water for at least 30 minutes to prevent them from burning during the cooking.

Ⓜ **Chicken Kebabs in Yogurt-Cumin Sauce** In Step 1, replace the marinade with 1 cup yogurt; 1 medium onion, minced; 1 tablespoon minced garlic; the minced zest and juice of 1 lime; 1 tablespoon ground cumin; ¼ teaspoon cayenne, or to taste; ½ teaspoon ground coriander; 1 teaspoon paprika; and salt and pepper to taste. Proceed.

Ⓜ **Chicken Kebabs with Citrus** In Step 1, replace the marinade with 2 tablespoons soy sauce; 1 tablespoon peanut or other oil; the minced zest and juice of 1 medium orange, 1 lemon, and 1 lime; 1 tablespoon peeled and minced fresh ginger; 1 tablespoon honey; 1 small onion, minced; and salt and pepper to taste. Proceed as in Step 2.

2 | Salads and Soups

 Make Ahead

Mesclun with Goat Cheese and Croutons

Make sure the goat cheese is at room temperature before serving (you may warm it gently in the oven if you like).

Makes 4 servings

Time: About 20 minutes

5 to 6 cups torn mixed greens (trimmed, washed, and dried)

Vinaigrette (at right)

4 Baked Croutons or Herb Croutons (at right), made without cubing the bread

4 ounces soft goat cheese, at room temperature, cut into quarters

 Toss the greens with the vinaigrette and divide among 4 plates.

 Spread the croutons with the goat cheese, and top each portion of greens with a crouton.

Shopping Tip: This is a good place for fresh goat cheese, something that is made locally in many communities throughout the country. But a slightly aged, camembert-like goat cheese is good here, too.

Ⓜ Vinaigrette

Makes 1 cup • Time: 5 minutes

You can emulsify the vinaigrette (blend until creamy) or not. Sometimes that extra creaminess is nice (and an immersion blender works brilliantly). But usually it doesn't matter much; I just toss everything in a bowl and whisk it for thirty seconds or so.

¼ cup good vinegar, such as sherry, balsamic, or high-quality red or white wine, plus more to taste

½ teaspoon salt, plus more if needed

½ teaspoon Dijon mustard (optional)

¾ cup extra-virgin olive oil, plus more if needed

2 teaspoons minced shallots (optional)

Freshly ground black pepper to taste

1 Briefly mix the vinegar, salt, and optional mustard with an immersion blender, food processor, or blender, or with a fork or wire whisk.

2 Slowly add the oil in a stream (drop by drop if whisking) until an emulsion forms; or just whisk everything together briefly. Add the remaining oil faster, but still in a stream.

3 Taste to adjust salt and add more oil or vinegar if needed. Add the shallots and pepper. This is best made fresh but will keep, refrigerated, for a few days; bring back to room temperature before using.

Ⓜ Baked Croutons

Makes about 2 cups cubes • Time: 20 to 40 minutes

If you like, rub the whole slices of bread with a cut clove of garlic before cooking.

**4 to 6 slices any bread, preferably
slightly stale**

1 Preheat the oven to 300°F. Cut the bread into cubes of any size, or leave the slices whole. Place them on a baking sheet.

2 Bake, shaking the pan occasionally if you used cubes, or turning the slices every 10 minutes or so if you left the slices whole. The croutons are done when they are lightly browned and thoroughly dried. Store in a covered container at room temperature for up to a week.

Ⓜ Herb Croutons

Makes about 2 cups cubes • Time: 10 to 15 minutes

Another simple crouton, my favorite for salads.

**4 tablespoons extra-virgin olive oil,
butter, or a combination**

**4 to 6 thick slices any bread,
cut into cubes if you like**

**2 teaspoons or more minced fresh herbs:
parsley, dill, chervil, thyme, or marjoram
alone, or any mixture of fresh herbs you
like**

Salt to taste

1 Place the olive oil or butter in a large skillet and turn the heat to medium. When the oil is hot or the butter melts, add the bread cubes and cook, stirring, until brown all over.

2 Add the herbs and continue to cook for 1 minute more. Remove and sprinkle lightly with salt. Store in a covered container at room temperature for up to a week.

Pear and Gorgonzola Salad

Something about this combination is magical: the smooth sweetness of the pears, the creamy saltiness of the cheese, the crunchiness of walnuts . . . it's a great salad for warm weather days or to lighten heavy holiday meals. Use any blue that you like—Gorgonzola, Roquefort, or Stilton, for example—as long as it's ripe and soft.

Makes 4 servings

Time: 20 minutes

---

1 cup walnut halves

4 to 6 cups torn mixed greens (trimmed, washed, and dried)

½ cup Vinaigrette (page 14)

2 pears, peeled, cored, and cut into slices

¼ pound Gorgonzola, Roquefort, or other good creamy blue cheese

1 Place the walnuts in a dry skillet and turn the heat to medium. Toast, shaking the pan frequently, until they are aromatic and beginning to darken in color, 3 to 5 minutes. Set aside to cool while you prepare the other ingredients.

2 Toss the greens with most of the vinaigrette and divide among 4 plates. Decorate with pear slices and crumble the cheese over all. Crumble or coarsely chop the walnuts and scatter them over the salad.

3 Drizzle with the remaining vinaigrette and serve.

Shopping Tips: Blue cheese can be made from the milk of goats, cows, or sheep. Goat blue has the distinctive flavor associated with all goat cheeses, and tends to be less creamy than the other two. The best-known blue sheep cheese is Roquefort. Usually, however, it's easier to find a good Gorgonzola or Stilton (both made from cow's milk), or a good domestic variety, like Maytag blue. Good blue cheese should be quite soft, though not runny.

Though some people like their pears as hard as apples, most prefer them soft, though not completely mealy. They're at their best when their "shoulders"—the part where they taper—yield readily to a firm touch.

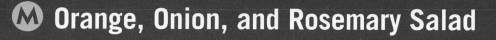 Orange, Onion, and Rosemary Salad

A simple, festive first course, which can be made year-round. Add some Niçoise, kalamata, or other good black olives to this if you like. And feel free to make it a bit in advance—in fact, it's best when made ahead, so the flavors can blend.

Makes 4 servings

Time: 15 minutes

---

4 navel oranges

1 small red onion

1 teaspoon minced fresh rosemary or ½ teaspoon dried rosemary, plus sprigs fresh rosemary for garnish (optional)

Salt and freshly ground black pepper to taste

2 tablespoons extra-virgin olive oil

1 Peel the oranges and section them (see illustrations below) or slice them thinly. Peel the onion and slice it thinly. Toss both with the minced fresh or dried rosemary, a small amount of salt and pepper, and the olive oil.

2 Serve immediately or refrigerate for up to 2 hours (bring to room temperature before serving). Garnish with rosemary sprigs, if you have them, before serving.

Peeling and Segmenting an Orange

(**Step 1**) Before beginning to peel and segment citrus, cut a slice off both ends of the fruit so that it stands straight. (**Step 2**) Cut as closely to the pulp of the fruit as possible, removing the skin in long strips. (**Step 3**) To segment citrus, use a paring knife to cut between the sections, leaving the membrane behind. (Or simply segment as you would a grapefruit.)

Seafood Salad, Adriatic-Style

The preparation of this dish takes some time, but there is nothing complicated about it. The biggest challenge lies in the shopping. Check with your fishmonger or your supermarket fish department a day or two in advance to make sure you can get what you want.

Makes 10 to 15 servings

Time: 2 hours, plus marinating time

---

8 cups fish or vegetable stock, store-bought broth, or water

Salt and freshly ground black pepper to taste

1 onion, cut in half but unpeeled, if using water

3 cloves garlic, lightly crushed, if using water

1 carrot, peeled and cut into chunks, if using water

½ bunch fresh parsley, if using water

2 bay leaves, if using water

1 tablespoon vinegar, if using water

½ cup dry white wine, if using water

About 3 pounds octopus, cleaned

3 pounds salmon fillet

3 pounds squid, cleaned, or use scallops

3 pounds medium-to-large shrimp, 15 to 30 per pound

1 to 2 pounds "Grilled" Sardines (at right)

4 cups cooked or canned white beans, drained

An assortment of vegetables: raw fennel, roasted red pepper, steamed carrots and/or new potatoes, and a mixture of washed and dried greens

Extra-virgin olive oil to taste

Lemon wedges

1. Bring the stock to a boil in a large pot, or instead simmer together 8 cups of water and the salt, pepper, onion, garlic, carrot, parsley, bay leaves, vinegar, and white wine for about 10 minutes; strain and discard solids.

2. Add the octopus and simmer until tender, at least 1 hour. Add the salmon and turn the heat to an absolute minimum; cook 3 minutes. Add the squid or scallops and the shrimp and cook until the shrimp begin to turn pink, 2 or 3 minutes. Turn off the heat and let the seafood cool in the water for 10 minutes.

3. Strain. Reserve the stock for another use (or use to poach vegetables for the salad). Shell the shrimp; cut the octopus, squid, and shrimp into bite-sized pieces.

4. Arrange the octopus, squid, and shrimp in small piles on a platter, along with the sardines, poached salmon, beans, and vegetables. Sprinkle all with salt and pepper. (You can cover and refrigerate at this point for a couple of hours, but let the salad return to room temperature before serving.)

5. To serve, drizzle everything with olive oil and pass the platter, along with more olive oil and lemon wedges.

"Grilled" Sardines

Makes 2 servings • Time: 15 minutes, plus time to preheat the broiler

Not grilled but broiled, as they are throughout Europe, where they are a popular appetizer. If you have a grilling basket, you can cook these over hot coals, but the broiler does a wonderful job. You can follow these directions for smelts, too. Serve as directed below with lemon wedges or use in Seafood Salad, Adriatic-Style (at left).

6 to 12 large sardines, a total of about 1 pound, gutted, with heads on, rinsed and dried well	Salt and freshly ground black pepper to taste
Melted butter or olive oil	Minced fresh parsley leaves for garnish
	Lemon wedges

1 Preheat the broiler. Brush the fish inside and out with butter or oil; sprinkle with salt and pepper. Lay them in a baking dish that can hold them, side by side, without crowding.

2 Broil the sardines, turning once, about 4 inches from the heat source, until browned on both sides, about 6 minutes total. (Sometimes these fish are too delicate to turn; just finish the cooking on the top side, moving them a little farther from the heat if necessary to prevent burning.) Garnish and serve with lemon wedges.

Carrot Salad with Cumin

Here's a simple salad in a typically North African style, one that can add both flavor and surprise to any holiday meal. It features carrots, complemented by the sweetness of fresh oranges and the tang of ground cumin.

Makes 4 servings

Time: 15 minutes

1½ pounds carrots, peeled and grated

Juice of 2 oranges

Juice of 1 lemon

2 tablespoons extra-virgin olive oil

Salt and freshly ground black pepper to taste

1 teaspoon ground cumin, or more to taste

1 Use the julienne cutter of a food processor to cut the carrots into fine shreds, or cut into ⅛-inch-thick slices.

2 Blend the remaining ingredients and pour the dressing over the carrots. Toss and serve.

Root Vegetables with Cumin This salad is equally good with grated celeriac, jicama, or sunchokes, for some (or even all) of the carrots, using the same dressing. Celeriac, a knobby, rough textured root, is closely related to celery and tastes like it; trim the exterior portions with a paring knife before using. Jicama is easier to peel, its flesh being somewhat smoother, but is also a large root. Sunchokes, also called Jerusalem artichokes, are neither from Jerusalem nor artichokes, but they're small, good tasting roots that come from a form of sunflower; peel before using.

Turkey (or Chicken) Soup with Rice or Noodles

This is a thin soup—a warming but not super-filling first course—with the rice, meat, and vegetables acting as a garnish rather than a major player. Use orzo or other tiny pasta, angel hair or other thin noodles, ribbons or other egg noodles, or other cooked grains in place of the rice. The stock can be made by simmering leftover scraps of turkey along with the carcass and some vegetables for an hour or two.

Like most soups, this one can be made a couple of days in advance, but you may have to thin it a bit before heating to serve because the rice (or pasta) will swell during storage.

Makes 4 servings

Time: 30 minutes

---

5 to 6 cups chicken stock
or store-bought broth

½ cup long-grain rice or pasta

1 carrot, peeled and cut into thin slices

1 celery stalk, minced (optional)

1 cup raw or cooked chopped boneless skinless turkey or chicken, or more

Salt and freshly ground black pepper to taste

Minced fresh parsley or dill leaves for garnish

1 Place the stock in a large, deep saucepan or casserole and turn the heat to medium-high. When it is just about boiling, turn the heat down to medium so that it bubbles but not too vigorously. Stir in the rice, carrot, and celery and cook, stirring occasionally, until they are all tender, about 20 minutes.

2 Stir in the meat. If it is raw, cook another 5 to 8 minutes, until it is cooked. If it is cooked, cook 2 or 3 minutes, until it is hot. Season with salt and pepper, garnish, and serve.

Preparation Tip: You can easily make stock with leftover turkey. Roast the meat and bones along with a few carrots or onions until browned. Then add water and simmer for about an hour. Cool, strain, and season with salt and pepper.

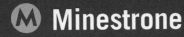 # Minestrone

Essentially, vegetable soup, best made with a little bit of prosciutto. Consider this recipe a series of suggestions, rather than something ironclad; you can make minestrone with any vegetables you have on hand. This can be made a couple of days ahead of time and reheated.

Makes 4 servings

Time: 45 minutes to 1 hour

4 tablespoons extra-virgin olive oil

1 medium onion, minced

1 carrot, peeled and diced

½ cup minced prosciutto or other ham (optional)

4 cups assorted mixed vegetables, cut into small cubes if necessary: potatoes, carrots, corn, peas, string beans, cooked dried beans (cranberry beans, or borlotti, are traditional), celery, zucchini or summer squash, pumpkin or winter squash, leeks, parsnips, turnips, etc.

Salt and freshly ground black pepper to taste

5 cups chicken, beef, or vegetable stock, store-bought broth, or water, preferably warmed

10 sprigs fresh parsley, more or less

1 cup cored, peeled, seeded, and chopped tomatoes (canned are fine; include their juice)

Freshly grated Parmesan cheese

1 Place 3 tablespoons of the oil in a large, deep saucepan or casserole and turn the heat to medium. A minute later, add the onion and carrot. Cook, stirring, until the onion softens, about 5 minutes. Add the ham if you're using it and cook, stirring, another 3 minutes.

2 Add the remaining vegetables, season with salt and pepper (go easy on the salt if you've included ham), and cook, stirring, for 1 minute. Add the stock or water, parsley, and tomatoes and turn the heat to medium-low. Cook, stirring every now and then, until the vegetables are very soft, about 30 minutes. (You may prepare the soup in advance up to this point. Cover, refrigerate for up to 2 days, and reheat before proceeding.)

3 Sprinkle with the remaining olive oil and serve, passing the cheese at the table.

Ⓜ **Beef and Vegetable Soup** Replace the ham with ½ pound minced beef (leftover beef stew is not only okay but preferable). Use beef stock if at all possible.

Creamy Pumpkin or Winter Squash Soup

A complex and interesting version of the winter classic; for a lighter version, see the variation. Make this a couple of days ahead if you like, but add the cream just before serving.

Makes 4 servings

Time: 45 minutes

3 tablespoons butter

1 pound pumpkin or winter squash, peeled, seeded, and cut into 1- to 2-inch cubes

1 pound crisp tart apples, such as McIntosh or Granny Smith, peeled, cored, and roughly chopped

1 large onion, roughly chopped

Salt and freshly ground black pepper to taste

4 cups chicken, beef, or vegetable stock, store-bought broth, or water, preferably warmed

1/2 cup dry white wine

1 teaspoon fresh tarragon leaves or 1/4 teaspoon dried tarragon

1 cup heavy or light cream

Minced fresh parsley leaves or snipped chives for garnish

1 Place the butter in a large, deep saucepan; turn the heat to medium. When it melts, add the pumpkin, apples, and onion. Cook, stirring, until the onion softens, 5 to 10 minutes. Season with salt and pepper.

2 Add the stock or water, wine, and tarragon; turn the heat to medium-high and bring to a boil. Turn the heat down to low, partially cover, and cook for about 30 minutes, until the pumpkin is very soft. Cool slightly, then puree the soup in a food mill or blender. (You may prepare the soup in advance up to this point. Cover, refrigerate for up to 2 days, and reheat before proceeding.)

3 Return it to the pan and cook gently over medium-low heat until heated through; do not boil. Stir in the cream and cook, stirring, until hot, about 1 minute (do not boil). Garnish and serve.

Shopping Tip: Unless you want a jack-o'-lantern, buy small pumpkins—3 pounds is big enough. Avoid those with soft spots. Store at room temperature or refrigerate for up to a month.

Preparation Tip: Use a cleaver or very large knife to split the pumpkin in half or cut wedges. Scoop out the seeds and strings and discard. To peel, use a paring knife, and don't fret if you take a fair amount of the flesh with the skin; it's unavoidable.

Easy Winter Squash Soup Combine the pumpkin or squash with salt, pepper, and 4 to 6 cups stock. Cook until the squash is very soft, then cool and puree. Reheat, with or without cream (or milk, sour cream, or yogurt). Taste and adjust seasoning, then garnish with chives or parsley and serve.

No-Holds-Barred Clam or Fish Chowder

This can be a special dish if your fish is lobster. It becomes corn chowder simply by substituting 1 cup (or more) of fresh corn kernels for the clams or fish. Better still, just add some fresh corn along with the fish. I sometimes use flour in this recipe, simply because most people are used to very thick chowders; but it isn't necessary.

Makes 4 servings

Time: 30 minutes

4 to 6 slices good bacon (about ¼ pound), minced

1 cup minced onion

2 cups peeled and roughly chopped baking potatoes

2 tablespoons flour (optional)

1 teaspoon fresh thyme leaves
or ½ teaspoon dried thyme

2 cups any fish stock, or store-bought chicken broth, augmented by as much juice as you can salvage when opening the clams

Salt and freshly ground black pepper to taste

1 cup milk

1 cup heavy cream or half-and-half or more milk

24 hard-shell clams, shucked; or about 1 pint shucked clams, cut up if very large, with their juice; or about 2 cups diced or chunked fresh delicate white fish, such as cod or lobster

1 tablespoon butter

Minced fresh parsley leaves for garnish

1 Fry the bacon in a large, deep saucepan or casserole over medium-high heat until crisp. Remove with a slotted spoon and cook the onion and potatoes in the bacon fat until the onion softens, 10 minutes. Sprinkle with the optional flour and the thyme and stir. Add the stock and cook until the potatoes are tender, about 10 minutes. (You may prepare the soup in advance up to this point. Cover, refrigerate for up to 2 days, and reheat before proceeding.)

2 Add salt and pepper, then the milk and cream; add the clams or fish and bring barely to a simmer over low heat. Float the butter on top of the chowder; by the time it melts, the clams or fish will be ready. Garnish and serve.

Shucking Clams

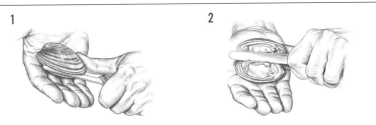

1   2

To open a clam, you must use a blunt, fairly thick knife; there is a knife made specifically for this purpose (called, not surprisingly, a "clam knife"), and it's worth having for this chore. **(Step 1)** Hold the clam in your cupped hand, and wedge the edge of the knife into the clam's shell opposite the hinge. Once you get it in there the clam will give up all resistance. **(Step 2)** Run the knife along the shell and open up the clam. Try to keep as much juice inside the shell as you can. Detach the meat from the shell and serve.

One-Hour Bouillabaisse

This is the most basic bouillabaisse: a mess of fish cooked in broth. There is little reason to make a bigger deal of this essentially simple stew than this. Serve, if you like, with Aioli (page 31).

Makes 6 to 8 servings

Time: About 1 hour

4 tablespoons extra-virgin olive oil

1 large onion, chopped

3 cored, peeled, seeded, and chopped tomatoes (canned are fine; include their liquid)

2 or 3 ribbons orange zest, removed from an orange with a vegetable peeler

1 teaspoon fennel seeds

1 teaspoon minced fresh tarragon leaves or ¼ teaspoon dried tarragon

5 sprigs fresh parsley

4 cups fish or chicken stock, store-bought broth, or water, warmed

12 slices crusty French bread

1 clove garlic, split in half, plus 1 tablespoon minced garlic

24 small hard-shell clams or mussels, well washed

1½ pounds fillet or steak fish, preferably a combination of halibut, cod, snapper, and sea bass, cut into chunks

1½ pounds shellfish, preferably a combination of scallops and shrimp

¼ cup minced fresh basil leaves, plus more for garnish

1 tablespoon Pernod or other anise liqueur (optional)

Salt and freshly ground black pepper to taste

1 Place 3 tablespoons of the olive oil in a large, deep saucepan or casserole and turn the heat to medium-low. A minute later, add the onion and cook, stirring, until it softens, about 5 minutes. Add the tomatoes, orange zest, fennel seeds, tarragon, and parsley. Stir to blend. Preheat the oven to 350°F.

2 Add the stock, broth, or water and turn the heat to high. Bring to a boil, cover, and turn the heat to medium-low; cook for 10 minutes. While the broth simmers, toast the rounds of bread in the oven until dried (about 20 minutes). Rub the toasts with the split clove of garlic and put a piece of bread in as many soup bowls as there are diners. Reserve the remainder to pass at the table.

3 Add the clams to the broth and continue to cook, covered, for about 5 minutes. Add the fish fillets or steaks to the broth and cook another 5 minutes. When the first of the clams begins to open, add the shellfish to the broth along with the garlic, basil, Pernod, and the remaining tablespoon of olive oil. Season with salt and pepper.

4 Cover and cook for 3 to 5 minutes. Taste and adjust seasoning. Spoon some fish and broth into each bowl over the toasted French bread, garnish with a bit more basil, and serve.

Shopping Tips: Clams and mussels should be alive when you buy them. This will mean that hard-shell clams (littlenecks, cherrystones, quahogs, etc.) will have closed, undamaged shells that will be next to impossible to open with your hand. Mussels and soft-shell clams (steamers) will have gaping, undamaged shells that will move when you click them together.

Anise liqueur—Pernod and Ricard are the most common brands—is a strong-flavored drink from France, related to ouzo (Greece), raki (Turkey), and a handful of other such spirits. The flavor is traditional in bouillabaisse, and also makes a great drink, over ice, with a splash of water or soda.

3 | Fish

Ⓜ **Make Ahead**

Herb-Rubbed Swordfish, Tuna, or Other Steaks

A step forward in grilling, but still simple as can be, and astonishingly good. Tuna should be cooked quite rare, and even swordfish should not be cooked to well-done; it's best when a little pink and quite juicy. Other fish steaks you can try: mako and monkfish (not a true steak, but works well in steak recipes).

Makes 4 servings

Time: 45 minutes, plus time to preheat the grill

2 (1-inch-thick) swordfish or tuna steaks, a total of 1½ to 2 pounds

Salt and pepper to taste

1 tablespoon grated or minced lemon peel

1 large minced clove garlic

2 tablespoons minced mixed fresh herbs, such as parsley, chives, basil, sage, thyme, and/or rosemary.

Lemon wedges

4 Simple Ideas for Grilled Fish

1 Serve with any vinaigrette (Vinaigrette, page 14, or Walnut Oil Vinaigrette, page 55), Mayonnaise (page 31), or your favorite salsa.

2 Brush lightly with vinegar and rub lightly with spices or spice blends such as curry powder before grilling.

3 Serve hot on a lightly dressed salad.

4 Use (hot or cold) in a sandwich, with freshly squeezed lemon juice, or other dressing.

1 Start a charcoal or wood fire or preheat a gas grill or broiler; the fire should be quite hot and the rack should be fairly close to the heat, 3 or 4 inches at most.

2 Sprinkle the fish with salt and pepper, then combine the lemon peel, garlic, and herbs and rub this mixture into the fish. If you like, let rest for an hour or so (refrigerated if the room is warm).

3 Grill the fish. After 4 minutes, the fish should be nicely browned; turn it. Three minutes later, check the fish for doneness by peeking between the layers of flesh with a thin-bladed knife—when the knife meets little resistance and just a touch of translucence remains, the swordfish is done. Serve immediately, with the lemon wedges.

Grilled Swordfish, Tuna, or Other Steaks with Mustard Sauce This dish is great with boiled potatoes. Step 1 remains the same. In Step 2, omit the herb mixture. Instead, brush the fish with 1 tablespoon of olive or other oil, then sprinkle it with salt and pepper. Grill as in Step 3. Combine ¼ cup olive oil, 3 tablespoons Dijon mustard, ¼ cup minced shallots, 2 tablespoons minced fresh parsley leaves, 2 tablespoons freshly squeezed lemon juice, and salt and pepper to taste. Drizzle the steak with a bit of this, then pass the rest at the table. Omit the lemon wedges.

Salmon Roasted in Butter

If you make this with the most flavorful, beautiful fillet you can find—such as Alaskan sockeye in season, or a lovely side of farm-raised salmon—you will be amazed by the richness of flavor. The simplicity of this dish allows you to make a special meal quickly or to spend extra time and energy on accompanying dishes.

Makes 4 to 8 servings

Time: 15 minutes

---

4 tablespoons (½ stick) butter

1 (2- to 3-pound) salmon fillet, skin on (but scaled) or off, pin bones removed (see below)

Salt and freshly ground black pepper to taste

Minced fresh parsley leaves for garnish

Removing Pin Bones

(Step 1) Fillets of many fish, no matter how skillfully removed, may contain long bones along their center, which must be removed by hand. Feel with your fingers to see if your fillet contains pin bones.

(Step 2) Remove them with a needle-nose pliers or similar tool.

1 Preheat the oven to 475°F. Melt the butter in a medium roasting pan—either on top of the stove or in the oven as it preheats—until the foam subsides.

2 Place the salmon in the butter, flesh side down, and put the pan in the oven. Roast about 5 minutes, then turn and roast 3 to 6 minutes longer, until the salmon is done (peek between the flakes with a thin-bladed knife). Sprinkle with salt and pepper, garnish, and serve immediately.

Shopping Tip: Farm-raised salmon (it's usually Atlantic salmon) is available year-round and is fairly flavorful and usually inexpensive. Wild salmon, from the Pacific Northwest, is only available fresh from spring to fall, but it's preferable, especially if you can find king (chinook), sockeye (red), or coho (silver). Chum and pink salmon are less valued but still good wild varieties.

Preparation Tip: Few supermarkets will scale salmon fillets for you, so the easiest thing to do is to cook the fish with the scales on and simply peel off the skin (which takes almost no effort once the fish is cooked). This works well, because the scales give added protection against overcooking, and come right off with the skin.

Cooking Tip: The cooking time for salmon varies according to your taste. I prefer my salmon cooked to what might be called medium-rare to medium, with a well-cooked exterior and a fairly red center. So, I always look at the center of a piece of salmon to judge its doneness. Remember that fish retains enough heat to continue cooking after it has been removed from the heat source, so stop cooking just before the salmon reaches the point you'd consider it done.

Cold Poached Salmon with Dill Mayonnaise

This poaching method is easy and consistently results in a moist piece of fish without a lot of fuss. Note that the fish can be poached a day in advance.

Makes 4 to 6 servings

Time: 30 minutes, plus time to cool

---

1 whole salmon, 3 pounds or larger, gutted, gilled, and scaled, or 1 (3-pound) cross-cut section from a larger salmon, or 1 large (3-pound) fillet, skin on (but scaled), pin bones removed (page 29)

2 heaping tablespoons salt

Mayonnaise (at right), preferably made with lemon juice (or use bottled mayonnaise)

½ cup or more snipped dill leaves

1 Place the salmon in a pot large enough to hold it (a deep roasting pan will work). Cover the salmon with cold water and use aluminum foil to make a lid for the pan. Add the salt and bring to a boil. Turn off the heat immediately and let the salmon sit in the hot water for 10 minutes for a fillet, up to 30 minutes for a large, whole fish. Check for doneness by peeking near the center bone, using a thin-bladed knife; do not overcook. Remove the fish from the water, drain, and chill. You can prepare the fish up to a day in advance if you like.

2 Meanwhile, make the mayonnaise and stir in dill to taste. To serve the salmon, insert the tine of a fork under the skin at the mid-line of each side of the fish, then run it lengthwise, splitting the skin. The skin will peel off easily. Take the salmon off the bone in the kitchen or at the table, using a spoon and following the natural contours of the fish. Serve with the mayonnaise.

Shopping Tip: Buying a whole salmon, once a challenge, has become a snap thanks to the presence of (almost) always-fresh farm-raised salmon. Call your fishmonger or supermarket a day ahead, because they may have to order one (most salmon is shipped already filleted); but they should have no trouble getting it.

Ⓜ Mayonnaise

Makes 1 cup • Time: 10 minutes

With the food processor or blender you can make perfect mayonnaise the first time you try it. Remember, however, you need a total of 2 tablespoons of liquid for the emulsion to work. If you don't have lemon juice, which is the perfect liquid, use mild vinegar (or dilute your vinegar with a little water).

1 egg or egg yolk

Dash cayenne

1/2 teaspoon dry mustard

Salt and freshly ground black pepper to taste

2 tablespoons freshly squeezed lemon juice, or white wine, rice, Champagne or other mild vinegar

1 cup extra-virgin olive oil, or canola or other neutral oil, or a combination, or more if needed

1 Combine the egg, cayenne, mustard, salt, pepper, lemon juice, and 1/4 cup of the oil in the container of a blender or food processor; turn on the machine and, with the machine running, add the oil in a thin, steady stream.

2 After you've added about half of the oil, the mixture will thicken; you can then begin adding the oil a bit faster. You can add up to 1 1/2 cups of oil and still have a pleasant, yellow (or pale yellow, if you included the egg white) mayonnaise. If the mixture is thicker than you'd like, add a little warm water, with the machine still running, or stir in a little cream or sour cream by hand. Check the seasoning and serve or store in the refrigerator for up to a week.

Ⓜ **Herb Mayonnaise** Add 1/4 cup or more of fresh herbs to the basic recipe, at the beginning. Start with parsley or chives, but experiment with dill, tarragon (smaller amounts, or mixed with parsley), basil, and so on. If you want rather green mayonnaise, start with the herb of your choice, and add at least 1/4 cup parsley to the mix.

Ⓜ **Aioli, or Garlic Mayonnaise** Serve with fish, or as a dip for vegetables, or as a sauce for any simple cooked food. Add 1 to 4 whole peeled cloves of garlic at the beginning. If you like, add a small (no larger than 1 inch thick in any direction) boiled and peeled potato to the mixture at the start for extra body. Thin as necessary with cream, stock, or water.

Ⓜ **Real Tartar Sauce** Stir 1/4 cup of minced sour pickles (preferably cornichons) and 1 tablespoon minced shallots or scallions into finished mayonnaise. Add prepared horse-radish to taste.

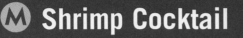

Shrimp Cocktail

Almost any shrimp recipe can be made into an appetizer, but this classic—among the best reasons to keep ketchup in the house—is never anything but. Cook the shrimp with shells on for maximum flavor, but peel before serving this as an appetizer. The shrimp can be cooked and chilled and the sauce made up to a day in advance.

Makes 4 servings

Time: 20 minutes

---

1 pound large shrimp, preferably with their peels on

½ cup ketchup

1 teaspoon chili powder

3 tablespoons freshly squeezed lemon juice

Salt and freshly ground black pepper to taste

1 tablespoon Worcestershire sauce, or to taste

Several drops Tabasco or other hot sauce

1 tablespoon prepared horseradish, or to taste

1 tablespoon finely minced onion (optional)

Iceberg lettuce (optional)

1 Place the shrimp in salted water to cover and turn the heat to high; when it boils, reduce the heat to medium-low and cook just until the shrimp are pink all over, 3 to 5 minutes. Turn off the heat and rinse immediately in cold water. Peel and, if you like, devein the shrimp (at right).

2 Combine all the other ingredients (except the lettuce); taste and adjust seasoning. If time allows, chill both shrimp and sauce.

3 Serve individual portions of shrimp, on a bed of lettuce if you like, with a small bowl of sauce.

Shopping Tips: Because almost all shrimp is frozen before sale, it makes some sense to buy still-frozen shrimp rather than those that have been thawed. Because the shelf life of previously frozen shrimp is not much more than a couple of days, buying thawed shrimp gives you neither the flavor of fresh nor the flexibility of frozen. Stored in the home freezer, shrimp retain their quality for a month or more.

Learn to judge shrimp size by the number it takes to make a pound, as retailers do. Shrimp labeled "16/20," for example, require 16 to 20 individual specimens to make a pound. Those labeled "U-20" require fewer (under 20) to make a pound. Shrimp of from 15 or 20 to about 30 per pound usually give the best combination of flavor, ease (peeling tiny shrimp is a nuisance), and value.

Preparation Tip: Shrimp should be peeled if it's to be cooked in a sauce that will make it difficult to peel them at the table. They might also be peeled if you're feeling generous or energetic. The shells, by the way, make a super broth. For simple grilling or pan-cooking, however, it's arguable that shrimp with their peels on lose less liquid and flavor.

Cooking Tip: Shrimp is among the easiest shellfish to cook. It isn't always done when it turns pink—some larger shrimp take a little longer to cook through—but it usually is. Cut one open to be sure.

Spicy Grilled or Broiled Shrimp

This is a great cocktail party dish, as it's easily served on toothpicks, and it's almost as quick to make with 6 pounds of shrimp as it is with 2. In any case, make plenty: This is the kind of dish that makes people eat more than they should.

Makes 4 servings

Time: 20 minutes, plus time to preheat the grill

1 large clove garlic

1 tablespoon coarse salt

1/2 teaspoon cayenne

1 teaspoon paprika

2 tablespoons olive oil

2 teaspoons freshly squeezed lemon juice

1 1/2 to 2 pounds shrimp, in the 20 to 30 per pound range, peeled, rinsed, and dried

Lemon wedges

1 Start a charcoal or gas grill or preheat the broiler; in any case, make the fire as hot as it will get and adjust the rack so that it is as close to the heat source as possible.

2 Mince the garlic with the salt; mix it with the cayenne and paprika, then make it into a paste with the olive oil and lemon juice. Smear the paste all over the shrimp. Grill or broil the shrimp, 2 to 3 minutes per side, turning once. Serve immediately or at room temperature, with lemon wedges.

Preparation Tip: Some people won't eat shrimp that isn't deveined. Others believe that the "vein," which is actually the animal's intestinal tract, contributes to flavor. I can neither detect the presence of the vein when it is left in nor notice its absence when it is removed, so I ignore it. Devein if you like.

Preparing Shrimp

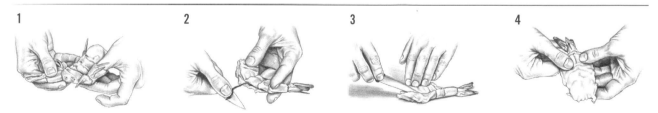

1   2   3   4

(Step 1) To peel shrimp, grasp the feelers on the underside and pull the peel away from the meat. (Step 2) Should you choose to devein, make a shallow cut on the back side of each shrimp, then pull out the long, black, threadlike vein. (Steps 3–4) To butterfly shrimp, cut most of the way through the back of the shrimp and open it up.

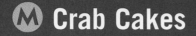
I like crab cakes that are mostly crab and seasonings, with a minimum of bread crumbs. When you buy "fresh" crabmeat (see Tip), it must be picked over for bits of shell or cartilage. The cakes can be made and shaped up to 24 hours before cooking them.

Makes 4 servings

Time: 15 minutes, plus refrigeration time

1 pound fresh lump or claw crabmeat, picked over for cartilage

1 egg

¼ cup minced red bell pepper

½ cup minced scallion

¼ cup Mayonnaise (page 31), or use prepared mayonnaise

1 tablespoon Dijon mustard

Salt and freshly ground black pepper to taste

2 tablespoons plain bread crumbs, or as needed

About 1 cup flour for dredging

1 teaspoon curry powder (optional)

2 tablespoons peanut, olive, or vegetable oil

2 tablespoons butter (or use all oil)

Lemon wedges and/or Real Tartar Sauce (page 31)

1 Mix together the crabmeat, egg, bell pepper, scallion, mayonnaise, mustard, salt, and pepper. Add sufficient bread crumbs to bind the mixture just enough to form into cakes; start with 2 tablespoons and use more if you need it.

2 Refrigerate the mixture until you're ready to cook (it will be easier to shape if you refrigerate it for 30 minutes or more, but it is ready to go when you finish mixing).

3 Season the flour with salt, pepper, and curry if you like. Preheat a large skillet, preferably non-stick, over medium-high heat for 2 or 3 minutes. Add the oil and butter and heat until the butter foam subsides. Shape the crabmeat mixture into 4 cakes, dredge each in the flour, and cook, adjusting the heat as necessary and turning once (very gently), until golden brown on both sides. Total cooking time will be about 10 minutes. Serve with lemon wedges and Tartar Sauce, if desired.

Shopping Tip: Most crabmeat is from the familiar 4- to 6-inch blue crab or—on the West Coast—rock or Dungeness crab. Often sold whole and live, crab is also cooked, its meat picked from the shell wherever it grows, to be sold throughout the country, refrigerated or frozen. When sold as picked meat, "lump" means large pieces from the body, "flake" means smaller pieces, but "claw" is best. Fresh crabmeat is expensive, but incredibly convenient and wonderfully flavorful; even with a squirt of lemon, it's celestial.

Crab Cakes with Lime-Ginger Sauce In place of the Real Tartar Sauce, make a dressing of 1 tablespoon peeled and grated ginger, 2 tablespoons peanut or other oil, 1 tablespoon soy sauce (or to taste), and 4 tablespoons lime juice (or to taste). Whisk together and spoon a little over each crab cake.

Baked Stuffed Clams

One of those dishes that is far better at home than in restaurants, because at home you're not interested in the filler, just accentuating the great taste of fresh clams. It's a Christmas Eve favorite.

Makes 4 to 6 appetizer servings

Time: About 30 minutes

---

12 hard-shell clams, each under 2 inches in diameter

1 tablespoon olive oil

1 tablespoon minced garlic

1 cup plain bread crumbs, preferably fresh

2 tablespoons minced fresh parsley leaves

Dash cayenne

Salt and freshly ground black pepper to taste

Freshly squeezed lemon juice if needed

Lemon wedges

Tabasco or other hot red pepper sauce to taste

1 Preheat the oven to 450°F. Shuck the clams, reserving half the shells and as much of the liquid as possible. (If you're not confident about shucking, steam the clams lightly, removing them the second their shells begin to open and preserving as much of their liquid as possible. You can also microwave, again removing them the second they begin opening.) Mince the clams (you can do this in a small food processor if you are careful; don't overprocess).

2 Heat the olive oil over medium heat in a medium skillet. Add the garlic and cook, stirring, just until it begins to color. Add the bread crumbs and cook, stirring, until the mixture browns. Add the parsley, cayenne, salt, and pepper. Stir and taste for seasoning. Add the reserved liquid and, if the mixture seems dry (or simply if you want a moister, more acidic mixture), some lemon juice. Add the minced clam meat. (You can stop here and refrigerate the stuffing for up to 24 hours before proceeding.)

3 Stuff the shells with this mixture, place them on a baking sheet or roasting pan, and bake until lightly browned, 10 to 15 minutes. Serve hot or warm, with lemon wedges and Tabasco.

Shopping Tip: Buying clams is easy, because those in the shell must be alive. When hard-shells die, you can move their shell apart; otherwise, they're shut up pretty tight, and you cannot even slide their shells from side to side. Live soft-shells (steamers) react visibly to your touch, retracting their necks and closing slightly (they are never closed all the way—hence the name "gapers"). Dead clams smell pretty bad, so it's unlikely you'll be fooled.

Preparation Tips: Store clams in a bowl in the refrigerator, where they will remain alive for several days.

Hard-shells—like littlenecks, quahogs, and cherrystones—require little more than a cleaning of their shells. I use a stiff brush to scrub them under running water. To shuck them, see the illustrated steps on page 24. Small hard-shells—under 2 inches across—are nice lightly steamed, like mussels, or stuffed and baked.

Boiled or Steamed Lobster

Should you boil or steam? It doesn't matter much. If you're cooking one batch of lobsters—whatever fits in your pot—steam them; it's much easier, and, because the lobster absorbs less water, far less messy. But lobsters flavor the cooking water (you should consider saving it as broth), which in turn flavors the lobsters. So if you're cooking a bunch, boil them. And eat the last of the batch yourself.

Makes as many servings as desired

Time: 30 minutes or less

---

1 (1½ pound or more) lobster per person or 1 (3 pound) lobster for two

Lemon wedges

1   In a large, covered pot (like one used for pasta), bring lots of water to a boil—or just 1 inch if you choose to steam—and add salt, a couple of handfuls or so (if you have access to clean seawater, that's a nice touch, as is steaming atop a pile of fresh seaweed).

2   Plunge the lobster(s) into the pot, cover, and cook about 8 minutes for its first pound—from the time the water returns to the boil—and then an additional 3 or 4 minutes per pound thereafter. Thus a 3-pounder should boil for 15 to 20 minutes. Lobster is done when the meat becomes opaque and firm, and the coral—which you only find in females—turns, well, coral-colored (it stays dark red until it is cooked). None of this does you any good if the lobster is whole, since you can't see or feel the meat or the coral. One assurance: It's difficult to undercook a small lobster, if you use the timing guidelines above. If you're boiling a larger one, insert an instant-read thermometer into the tail meat by sliding it in between the underside of the body and the tail joint; lobster is done at 140°F.

3   Remove the lobsters, which will be bright red, and let them sit for 5 minutes or so before serving. If lobsters have been boiled, poke a hole in the crosshatch right behind the eyes, and drain out the water. Eat. (The traditional accompaniment is drawn butter, but lobster is rich enough without it.) Try a squeeze of lemon.

Shopping Tips: When you're buying lobster, lift each one (make sure its claws are pegged or banded); if it doesn't flip its tail and kick its legs, look for another.

Two people sharing a 3-pound lobster will get more meat of equally high quality than if each eats a 1½-pound lobster. There's less work, less waste, and more meat hidden in those out-of-the-way places.

Broiled Lobster with Herb Stuffing

This is "baked stuffed lobster" as you've never had it in restaurants—the crisp, seasoned bread crumbs providing a nice foil for the sweet lobster meat.

Makes 4 servings

Time: 30 minutes

---

4 lobsters, about 1¼ pounds each

1 clove garlic, peeled

1 cup fresh parsley leaves

Salt and freshly ground black pepper to taste

2 cups plain bread crumbs, preferably homemade (at right)

¾ cup olive oil, plus more if needed

2 tablespoons freshly squeezed lemon juice, plus more if needed

1 Kill the lobsters as illustrated below; cut them in half, then remove the head sac. Remove and reserve the tomalley and coral (if any). Preheat the broiler and set the rack about 6 to 8 inches from the heat source.

2 In a food processor, combine the garlic, parsley, salt, pepper, bread crumbs, olive oil, lemon juice, and the tomalley and coral. Add a little additional olive oil or lemon juice if the mixture seems dry. Stuff the lobsters' body cavities with this mixture and broil until the tail meat is white and firm and the stuffing nicely browned, 5 to 10 minutes. (If the lobster is browning too quickly, either move it further from the heat source or turn off the broiler and turn the oven heat to 500°F to complete the cooking.)

Preparation Tip: To make bread crumbs, break fairly fresh or quite stale bread into chunks, and grind in a food processor or blender, a few chunks at a time. Toast crumbs on a baking sheet for 10 minutes in a 350°F oven, or store untoasted and toast, if you like, before using. Store bread crumbs in a sealed plastic bag in the freezer; they will keep forever.

Killing a Lobster

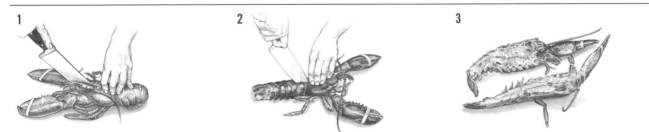

1   2   3

(Step 1) Before grilling or stir-frying, you can kill a lobster by parboiling it for a couple of minutes, or you can simply plunge a heavy knife right into the "crosshairs" behind the head. (Step 2) Cut up through the head and down through the tail. (Step 3) Your final product will look like this.

Sautéed Oysters

The best oysters should be eaten raw. (The tips and illustrations offer guidance on how to handle them.)To serve oysters on the half-shell, use any condiment you like. I prefer nothing at all (the great thing about oysters is their intense flavor), or at most a squeeze of lemon. But many people, especially those accustomed to large, dull-flavored oysters, prefer freshly ground black pepper; Tabasco sauce; or shrimp cocktail sauce (see Shrimp Cocktail, page 32).

Some oysters—especially those from the Deep South—are better cooked. And they're often sold preshucked, which eliminates almost all of the hassle of preparation. Frying fish at home, as noted elsewhere, is not as much fun as, for example, having someone do it for you. But pan-fried oysters are terrific, and not as messy.

Makes 4 appetizer servings or 2 main-course servings

Time: 30 minutes

---

2 eggs

¼ cup milk

Flour for dredging

Salt and freshly ground black pepper to taste

24 large shucked oysters, drained and dried

Plain bread crumbs for dredging

2 tablespoons olive or vegetable oil

2 tablespoons butter (or use all oil)

Lemon wedges

1 Beat the eggs lightly with the milk. Season the flour with salt and pepper. Dredge the oysters, one by one, in the flour, then dip in the egg mixture, then in the bread crumbs. Let them stand on waxed paper until you are ready to start cooking (you can refrigerate them for a few hours if you like).

2 Heat a large, deep skillet over medium-high heat for 2 or 3 minutes. Add the oil and butter. When the butter foam subsides, add the oysters, a few at a time. Do not crowd; you may have to cook in batches (and use more butter and oil). Cook, turning once, until browned on both sides, about 5 or 6 minutes total. Serve immediately, with lemon wedges.

Shucking Oysters

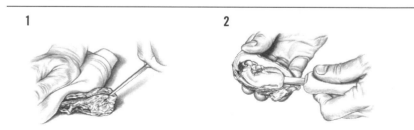

1   2

To open raw oysters, you can shuck them using an oyster knife, a can opener, or any sturdy (but preferably not too sharp) knife. The danger is in slipping, so protect your hand with a towel or glove. **(Step 1)** Place the oyster, cupped side down, on a flat surface and insert the knife into the hinge. Press and wiggle and twist that knife in there, until the oyster pops. Twist off the top shell, trying to keep as much juice inside as possible. **(Step 2)** Detach the meat from the shell and serve.

Shopping Tips: Oyster names are confusing, because they more often refer to where they're grown or harvested than what type they are: The Atlantic variety—also called Eastern—is almost always called by its place names, like Bluepoint, Wellfleet, and Apalachicola; the European oyster (the one most aficionados prefer)—also known as the "flat" (plat in French)—is sometimes called Belon, a name that belongs to a small region in France; the Pacific oyster, grown all over the world, is sometimes called a Portuguese ("Portugaise"), from a now-extinct species that once made up the majority of oysters grown in Europe.

If you're cooking oysters, the differences are less important. Use those that have been shucked, packaged, and marked with a "sell-by" date. But for oysters on the half-shell, you first have to determine which oyster you like (see above), and then make sure the shells are undamaged and shut tight.

Preparation Tips: To clean oysters, just scrub the shells thoroughly with a not-too-stiff brush. There's never any sand inside.

Shucking is the truly difficult part; see illustrations (at left), but also ask your fishmonger if he can do it for you. Keep them on a bed of crushed ice and eat them within a couple of hours.

21 Recipes Great for Last-Minute Entertaining

If you need hassle-free cooking when people are coming over during the holidays, plan a menu including some of these dishes that take 30 minutes or less to prepare.

4 | Poultry

Roast Chicken with Herb Butter

A simplified version of a classic that preserves the most important elements: a crisp-skinned chicken smacking of butter (or olive oil) and herbs. Easy enough for a weeknight, it's still quite special.

Makes 4 servings

Time: About 1 hour

---

8 tablespoons (1 stick) butter (preferred) or extra-virgin olive oil

1 tablespoon chopped fresh dill, tarragon, parsley, or chervil leaves, or a combination

Salt and freshly ground black pepper to taste

1 whole (3- to 4-pound) chicken, trimmed of excess fat, then rinsed and patted dry with paper towels

½ cup dry white wine or water, plus a little more if needed

1 clove garlic, lightly smashed (optional)

Minced fresh herbs for garnish

1 Preheat the oven to 450°F.

2 Using a fork, small food processor or blender, or potato masher, mash half the butter together with the herb(s), salt, and pepper. Loosen the skin of the chicken wherever you can, and spread some of this mixture between skin and meat, in the chicken cavity, and on top of the breast of the bird. Sprinkle the outside of the bird with more salt and pepper.

3 Put the remaining butter in a casserole or roasting pan and place the pan in the oven. When the butter has melted and its foam subsided, add the wine and the optional garlic. Place the chicken, breast side down, on a rack in the pan.

4 After the chicken has roasted for about 20 minutes, spoon some of the butter mixture over it, then turn the bird breast side up. (If, at any point, the pan juices are beginning to stick to the pan, add a little more liquid.) Baste again, then again after 7 or 8 minutes; at this point the breast should be beginning to brown (if it hasn't, roast a few more minutes). Turn the heat down to 325°F, baste again, and roast until an instant-read thermometer inserted into the thickest part of the thigh reads 160° to 165°F. Total roasting time will be under 1 hour.

5 Before removing the chicken from the pan, tip the pan to let the juices from the bird's cavity flow into the pan (if they are red, cook another 5 minutes). Remove the bird to a platter and let it rest for about 5 minutes before carving. Garnish with minced herbs and serve with the pan juices.

Roast Chicken with Herb Butter and Wine Sauce Steps 1–4 remain the same. In Step 5, while the bird is resting, place the roasting pan on a burner over high heat. Add 1 cup dry white wine and cook, stirring and scraping the bottom of the pan to loosen any solids that have stuck there, until the liquid is reduced by about half. Add 1 tablespoon of the minced fresh herb you have been using (less if you used tarragon), stir again, and serve with the chicken.

Roast Capon with Bacon-Nut Stuffing

Bigger than a chicken, and smaller than a turkey, capon offers something a little different for a special meal. You can use this stuffing with a roasting chicken, or with turkey, although chances are good you'll have to double or triple the quantities.

Makes at least 6 servings

Time: About 2 hours

$1/2$ pound slab or sliced bacon

3 tablespoons butter or oil (optional)

3 cups chopped onions

1 teaspoon minced garlic

2 cups unseasoned bread crumbs

$1/2$ cup pine nuts or chopped walnuts

$1/2$ cup dry white wine, chicken or vegetable stock, store-bought broth, or water

1 teaspoon fresh thyme leaves or $1/2$ teaspoon dried thyme, plus several sprigs of fresh thyme if available

1 bay leaf

Salt and freshly ground black pepper to taste

1 (6- to 7-pound) capon, trimmed of excess fat, then rinsed and patted dry with paper towels

2 carrots, chopped

1 cup water, stock, or store-bought chicken broth

1. If you are using slab bacon, cut it into $1/2$-inch cubes; if you're using sliced bacon, chop it coarsely. Cook the bacon in a medium skillet over medium heat, stirring or turning, until crisp. Drain, dry, and crumble; reserve the fat.

2. Heat 3 tablespoons of the bacon fat (or use butter or olive oil) over medium heat in a large, deep skillet. Cook 2 cups of the chopped onions, stirring, until softened, about 5 minutes. Add the garlic, bread crumbs, nuts, wine or stock, thyme, bay leaf, and bacon, and remove from the heat. Season to taste with salt—you may not need any—and pepper.

3. Preheat the oven to 425°F. Fill the capon with the stuffing. (Wrap and secure the legs with kitchen twine if you like or simply close the rear vent with metal skewers to keep the stuffing from falling out.) Set the bird on a rack in a roasting pan, brush it with a little of the bacon fat, some melted butter, or some olive oil, and sprinkle it with salt and pepper. Scatter the remaining onion, carrots, and thyme sprigs around the bird and place it in the oven.

4. Roast, basting every 10 minutes, first with butter or fat, then with pan juices. After 30 minutes, lower the heat to 350°F. Continue to baste every 15 minutes or so. The total cooking time will be $1 1/2$ to 2 hours. When the bird is done, an instant-read thermometer inserted into the thigh will measure about 165°F, and the juices will run clear rather than pink.

5. Transfer the bird to a hot platter. Spoon off most of the fat from the pan and place the pan over one or two burners on your stove. Turn the heat to high, add the water or stock, bring to a boil, and cook, stirring and scraping the bottom of the pan, until the liquid is reduced slightly, about 2 minutes. Season to taste. Carve capon and serve with stuffing and gravy.

Roast Turkey and Gravy

Basting helps improve the color and especially the flavor of the skin (though it really doesn't add any moisture to the bird's interior). For cooking time, use the chart at right or figure 15 minutes per pound. For example, an 8-pound bird will take about 2½ hours; a 16-pound bird should take just about 4 hours. Timing varies considerably, however, based on the frequency of basting and how much heat your oven loses, the original temperature of the turkey, and other factors. Your best bet for determining doneness is an instant-read thermometer, which should read 165° to 170°F in the thickest part of the thigh before you remove the bird from the oven. For stuffing options, see pages 80–81.

Makes 4 servings

Time: 2½ to 5 hours, depending on the size of the bird

---

1 (8- to 20-pound) turkey, with giblets

1 whole onion, plus 1 to 2 cups chopped onions

1 whole carrot, unpeeled, halved if large, plus 1 to 2 cups peeled and chopped carrots

Stems from 1 bunch parsley

½ teaspoon salt

Freshly ground black pepper to taste

8 tablespoons (1 stick) butter, melted, or extra-virgin olive oil, approximately

½ to 1 cup chopped celery

About 1 cup chicken stock, store-bought broth, or water, plus more as needed

¼ cup cornstarch mixed with ½ cup cold water (per 3 cups gravy) (optional)

1 Make sure the turkey is thoroughly defrosted before starting. Preheat the oven to 350°F. Combine the turkey neck, wing tips, and gizzard (but discard the liver) in a medium saucepan. Add the whole onion, whole carrot, and parsley stems. Add water to cover, ½ teaspoon salt, and a few grindings of pepper. Bring to a boil, turn the heat to low, and simmer, adding water as necessary to keep the meat and vegetables covered. Skim any foam that arises to the top of the pot; after 1 hour of simmering, turn off the heat, cover, and refrigerate if the turkey will cook for a great deal longer. Reheat when you get to Step 5.

2 Fit a large roasting pan with a V-shaped rack if you have one; otherwise use a flat rack. Brush the turkey with 1 tablespoon of the butter or oil and sprinkle it with salt and pepper. Place the turkey breast side up and scatter the chopped onions, carrots, and celery around it. Drizzle with 1 tablespoon of the butter or oil. Pour in about 1 cup of stock or water.

3 Roast, basting with a little additional butter or oil every 30 minutes and adding stock or water to the vegetables to keep them moist (better too wet than too dry in this case; you won't be eating them anyway). If you started the turkey with the breast down, flip it after an hour or so.

4 When the bird has about 1 hour of cooking to go (the internal temperature will be about 125°F), if the breast is not sufficiently browned (and it certainly won't be if you tented it with foil), turn the oven heat up to 400°F for the remaining cooking time. If at any time the bird appears to be browning too quickly, turn the heat back down (you can prop open the oven door for a couple of minutes to hasten the oven's cooling).

5 When the bird is done—an instant-read thermometer should read at least 165°F when inserted in mid-thigh—remove the bird to a platter but don't carve it until it has rested for at least 15 minutes. Reheat the giblet stock if necessary, then strain it into a bowl; then strain the vegetables that cooked with the bird into a larger bowl, pushing on them to extract as much liquid as possible. Combine these liquids. Mince the reserved liver.

6 Place the roasting pan over two burners on your stove, turn the heat to medium-high, and add 2 cups of the combined liquid and the reserved liver. Cook, stirring and scraping the bottom of the pan, until the liquid is reduced slightly. If your bird is small, season the gravy to taste and serve. If it is large, add as much more stock (using hot water to stretch it if necessary) as you like. If you want thicker gravy, combine 1/4 cup cornstarch with 1/2 cup cold water (per 3 cups of gravy) and stir it into the gravy until thickened.

7 Carve the turkey (page 46) and serve with the gravy.

Timing Guide for Roasting Turkey and Other Large Birds

Weight	Roasting Time (Unstuffed)	Roasting Time (Stuffed)
6–8 pounds	2–2½ hours	2½–3 hours
10–12 pounds	3–3½ hours	4 hours+
14–18 pounds	3½–4 hours	5–6 hours
18 pounds+	4 hours+	6 hours+

Choosing a Turkey

Here's my view on the kinds of turkeys out there, including standard, kosher, free-range, self-basting (such as Butterball), and "wild":

Standard This often amazingly cheap bird is versatile and, well, standard. Until something better comes along, this is often the best bet.

Kosher Somewhat better in flavor and texture than standard birds, at about twice the price. Usually sold frozen, although increasingly seen fresh at Thanksgiving. Worth a try.

Free-range In theory, a better bird than the standard, but, in fact, wildly inconsistent in quality and often outrageously expensive. If you can, find a local source, and, if it's good and reasonably priced, stick to it.

Self-basting Though not terrible in concept— because turkey meat is inevitably dry, an internal load of fat makes some sense—they are terrible in execution; the added ingredients used don't add anything good to the flavor.

"Wild" turkey True wild turkeys exist, of course, but you're not going to get one unless you or a friend shoots it yourself. The "wild" turkeys sold by mail-order houses and specialty stores are domesticated. They're quite expensive, not especially flavorful, and generally pretty tough.

Carving Turkey

1   **2**

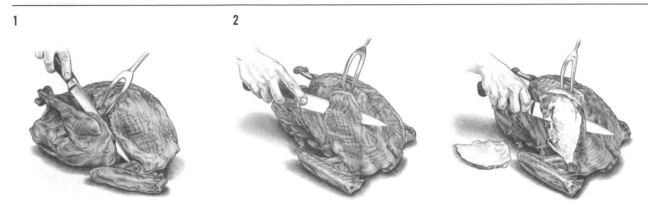

First, remove the leg-thigh section by cutting straight down between the leg and carcass, and through the joint holding the thigh to the carcass. Set aside for the moment.

At this point you have two options: Either cut thick slices of white meat from the breast, or remove the breast entirely from the carcass and slice it as you would a boneless roast.

3   **4**

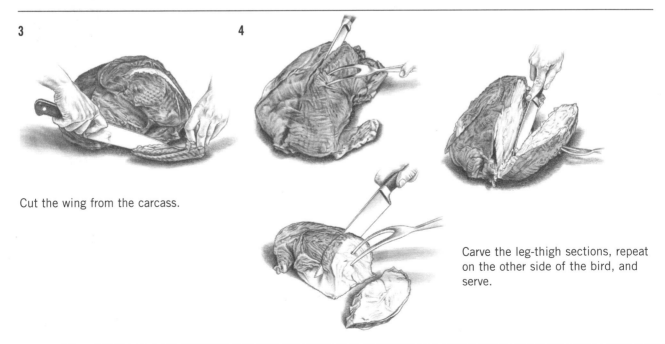

Cut the wing from the carcass.

Carve the leg-thigh sections, repeat on the other side of the bird, and serve.

Roast Turkey Breast, on the Bone

At 3 to 6 pounds, a turkey breast can feed a small party or a small group for a holiday. It can also give plenty of leftovers for Turkey Soup (page 21) or turkey sandwiches made with real turkey. And the roasting is a breeze. You can also use the variation for whole roast chicken on page 42, adjusting cooking time accordingly.

Makes 8 or more servings

Time: About 1 hour

---

1 (3- to 6-pound) turkey breast

About 3 tablespoons olive oil or melted butter for basting

Salt and freshly ground black pepper to taste

1 Preheat the oven to 450°F. Place the turkey on a rack in a roasting pan.

2 Brush the turkey with oil or butter and season it with salt and pepper. Place it in the oven. Roast for about 45 minutes, basting every 15 minutes or so, then begin checking every few minutes with an instant-read thermometer. The turkey is ready when the thermometer reads 160°F. Let the turkey rest for 5 to 10 minutes before carving and serving.

---

3 Simple Ways to Flavor Roast Turkey (or Other Birds)

1 Use freshly squeezed lemon juice in addition to or in place of olive oil.

2 Combine 2 tablespoons to 1/3 cup any mustard with 2 tablespoons honey and baste the bird with this mixture during the final stages of roasting. (Double the quantity for a large bird.)

3 Place 1/2 cup white wine and 2 cloves crushed garlic in the bottom of the roasting pan, baste with this in addition to or in place of the olive oil mixture above. (Double the quantity for a large bird.)

Roast Duck

Duck is fatty—amazingly so, if you're used to chicken—which means it needs to be treated differently from other birds. It also means it develops a beautifully crisp, dark skin. But although it is festive and almost invariably gorgeous, it doesn't serve a lot of people. So it's best for an intimate dinner, or one with plenty of side dishes.

Makes 2 to 4 servings

Time: About 1¼ hours

---

1 (4- to 5-pound) duck, excess fat removed, rinsed and patted dry with paper towels

Salt and freshly ground black pepper to taste

1 tablespoon soy sauce (optional)

1 Preheat the oven to 350°F. Prick the duck skin all over with a sharp fork, skewer, or thin-bladed knife; try not to hit the meat (the fat layer is usually about ¼ inch thick). Season the duck with salt and pepper and place it, breast side down, on a rack in a roasting pan.

2 Roast the duck for 15 minutes, prick the exposed skin again, then roast another 15 minutes. Brush with a little soy sauce, if desired, and then turn it breast side up. Prick again, brush with a little more soy sauce, then roast until the meat is done, about another 45 minutes; all juices, including those from the center vent, should run clear, and the leg bone should wiggle a little in its socket. When the bird is done, an instant-read thermometer inserted into the thigh will measure about 180°F. Raise the heat to 400°F for the last 10 minutes of cooking if the duck is not as brown as you'd like. (Reserve the fat in the pan for other uses.) Carve the duck (see illustration below) and serve.

Carving Small Roast Birds

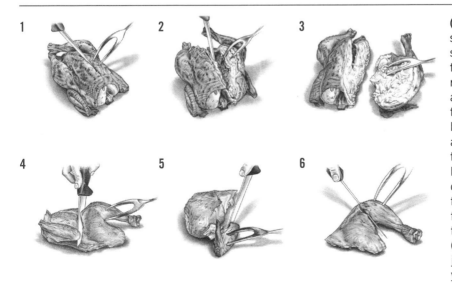

(Step 1) Cut straight down on either side of the breastbone, following the shape of the carcass. (Step 2) Continue to cut down toward the back until you reach the joints holding the thigh and wing to the carcass. (Step 3) Cut through those joints to free the entire half of the bird. (Step 4) Separate leg and breast sections by cutting through the skin that holds them together; hold the knife almost parallel to the cutting board, cut from the breast toward the leg, and you will easily find the right spot. (Step 5) Separate the wing from the breast if you like. (Step 6) Separate leg and thigh; the joint will offer little resistance once you find it.

Roast Goose

There is nothing better looking on the holiday table than a goose but, like duck, goose does not serve many people per pound. Its rich, dense meat is enormously satisfying, though, and the skin makes the effort worth it. If you plan to serve lots of people, figure about 6 servings; you can easily stretch it, though, with a few side dishes. One way to stretch the goose is to stuff it as you would a turkey, using any of the stuffings on pages 80–81.

Makes 6 to 10 servings

Time: About 2½ hours

---

1 (8- to 10-pound) goose, excess fat removed, rinsed and patted dry with paper towels

Salt and freshly ground black pepper to taste

1 Preheat the oven to 350°F. Prick the goose skin all over with a sharp fork, skewer, or thin-bladed knife; try not to hit the meat (the fat layer is usually about ¼ inch thick). Season the goose with salt and pepper and place it, breast side down, on a rack in a roasting pan.

2 Put the roasting pan in the oven and roast the goose for 20 minutes, prick the exposed skin again, then roast another 20 minutes, or until it begins to brown. Then turn the goose breast side up, prick again, and baste with some of the accumulated pan juices (there will be plenty). Roast for another hour, pricking the skin and basting two or three times during that period.

3 Unless the goose is already very brown, raise the heat to 400°F and continue to roast until the meat is done, about another 30 minutes. At that point, all juices, including those from the center vent, should run clear, and the leg bone should wiggle a little in its socket. When the bird is done, an instant-read thermometer inserted into the thigh will measure about 180°F.

4 Carve (at left) and serve.

Shopping Tip: Goose is nearly always sold frozen; you order it in advance then thaw it yourself. The easiest way to thaw goose is to let it sit in the refrigerator for 2 days before you plan to cook it. If you're in a hurry, defrost it by letting it sit in cold water, changing the water occasionally; but you should still plan for it to take the better part of a day for a 10-pound bird.

5 | Meat

Ⓜ Make Ahead

Prime Rib Roast for a Small Crowd

This is a simple roasting technique: high heat to sear the meat, lower heat to cook it through. If you want a really crisp exterior, turn the heat back to 450°F for a few minutes right at the end of cooking; this won't affect the internal temperature too much. Large roasts like this will cook more quickly if they are at room temperature before roasting.

Makes about 6 servings

Time: About 1½ hours, largely unattended

---

1 (3-rib) roast, about 5 pounds, trimmed of excess but not all fat

Salt and freshly ground black pepper to taste

1 or 2 cloves garlic (optional)

1 cup red wine, stock, store-bought broth, or water

1 Bring the meat to room temperature by removing it from the refrigerator at least an hour before cooking, preferably two. Preheat the oven to 450°F.

2 Place the meat, bone side down, in a large roasting pan. Season it with salt and pepper. If you like garlic, peel the cloves and cut them into tiny slivers; use a boning or paring knife to poke small holes in the meat and insert the garlic into them.

3 Place the roast in the oven and cook for 15 minutes, undisturbed. Turn the heat down to 350°F and continue to roast for about 1 hour; check in several places with a meat thermometer. When no spot checks in at under 125°F (120°F if you like your meat really rare and your guests are of the same mentality), the meat is rare; cook another 5 or 10 minutes if you like it better done, then check again, but in no case let the temperature of the meat go above 155°F.

4 Remove the meat from the oven (cover the meat with foil to keep it warm). Pour off all but a few tablespoons of the fat and place the roasting pan over a burner set to high. Add the liquid and cook, stirring and scraping up any brown bits, until it is reduced by half. Slice the roast and serve, splashing a little of the sauce on the meat platter and passing the rest at the table.

Shopping Tips: If you want the best roast, make a special request for the small end (the 12th through the 7th ribs) and ask the butcher—even a supermarket butcher can do this—to cut it to order for you, removing the short ribs; you want what's called a "short" roast.

If you are serving 4 to 6 people, buy 3 or 4 ribs (higher numbers are better, so look for ribs 12 through 10, or 9); if you're serving more, add another rib for every 2 people, unless you want to serve gargantuan portions. I usually buy a 3-rib roast for up to 6 people and have leftovers, but I believe in serving lots of side dishes when I make a roast so no one is tempted to eat a pound of meat.

Cooking Tips: For rare meat, figure about 15 to 20 minutes per pound roasting for any prime rib roast, regardless of the size, but see the recipe for details. All beef is rare at 125°F (120°F for really rare); there are noticeable differences in meat color for each 5° difference in temperature. I'd never cook anything beyond 155°F, although some cooks suggest cooking roast beef to 170°F for well done. Large roasts will rise at least 5° in temperature between the time you remove them from the oven and the time you carve them.

Cutting into a piece of meat to check its doneness is far from a sin; it's one of those things that everyone does but no one talks about. So if you're at all in doubt, cut into the middle or take a slice from the end. Your presentation will not be as beautiful but if the meat is perfectly cooked no one will care.

Prime Rib for a Big Crowd With bigger roasts, 5 ribs or more, make sure to allow plenty of time to let the meat reach room temperature. In Step 2, use more garlic if you like. In Step 3, increase initial browning time to 20 minutes. After that, cooking instructions remain the same, and cooking time will be only marginally longer, but be sure to use an instant-read thermometer in several different places to check the meat. Increase the liquid in Step 4 to at least 2 cups.

Carving a Rib Roast

For a bone-in prime rib, cut close to the bone, between the ribs, for the first slice.

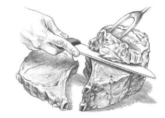

Unless you want huge portions, the second slice is boneless.

Roast Tenderloin with Herbs

A large piece of beef tenderloin makes a beautiful presentation. It's tender as can be, but not super-flavorful, so the herbs and a sauce are really essential.

Makes at least 10 servings

Time: At least 1½ hours, largely unattended

½ cup extra-virgin olive oil

1 tablespoon balsamic or sherry vinegar

¼ cup roughly chopped fresh parsley, stems included

1 teaspoon fresh thyme leaves, or several thyme sprigs, or ½ teaspoon dried thyme

1 bay leaf

2 cloves garlic, lightly smashed

1 (5-pound) tenderloin, trimmed of fat

Salt and freshly ground black pepper to taste

Walnut Oil Vinaigrette (at right)

1   Combine the first six ingredients; marinate the meat in this mixture for an hour or more (refrigerated if longer than an hour). When you're ready to cook, preheat the oven to 450°F.

2   Remove the meat from the marinade and pat it dry. Roast for 20 minutes, then check with meat thermometer; when the meat measures 125°F in a couple of places (since the thickness doesn't vary much, there shouldn't be much change in temperature from one spot to another) it is medium-rare; remove the roast from the oven and season with salt and pepper.

3   Let the meat rest for about 5 minutes before carving; cut into thick (at least ½ inch) slices, and serve with Walnut Oil Vinaigrette.

Roast Sirloin Strip   You can use anything from a 3- to a 10-pound (whole) strip; here, the weight won't affect cooking time much, because there is no bone and the thickness is uniform. Cook exactly as above, beginning to check temperature after 45 or 50 minutes; marinating and saucing are unnecessary, but a reduction sauce is quite nice: Simply pour out all but a bit of the fat from the roasting pan, then put it on the stove over high heat. Add 2 cups of fruity red wine and cook, stirring and scraping, until reduced by at least 50 percent. Season to taste and, if you like, stir in a bit of butter to smooth out the sauce. Serve with the meat.

(M) Walnut Oil Vinaigrette

Makes about ¾ cup • Time: 5 minutes

I find that the strong, wonderful flavor of walnut oil allows me to use less of it in a dressing. But remember—the ratio of oil to vinegar is as much a function of taste as of chemistry.

¼ cup sherry, balsamic, or good red wine vinegar

½ teaspoon salt

1 teaspoon Dijon mustard (optional)

½ cup walnut oil, plus a little more if needed

2 teaspoons minced shallots (optional)

Freshly ground black pepper to taste

1 Briefly mix the vinegar, salt, and mustard with an immersion blender, food processor or blender, or fork or wire whisk. Slowly add the oil in a stream (drop by drop if whisking) until an emulsion forms.

2 Add the remaining oil faster, but still in a stream. Taste to adjust salt and add more oil if needed. Add the shallots and pepper. This is best made fresh but will keep, refrigerated, for a few days; bring back to room temperature before using.

Braised Beef Brisket

Brisket becomes reasonably tender as long as it is cooked for a long time, with plenty of moisture. My favorite seasonings for it are very, very basic: the taste of the meat itself, some spices, and onions simmered in butter; a little bit of tomato is also nice. I serve brisket made this way, over broad noodles. But brisket is also great seasoned with bolder spices, or with sweet fruits and vegetables; see the variations.

Two technical points: You can skip the initial browning if you're pressed for time or don't want to bother; the difference, in the end, will be minimal. And although it's tempting to shred brisket along the grain, it makes a nicer presentation if sliced against the grain; use a very sharp carving knife and you can get beautiful, thin slices.

Makes 10 or more servings

Time: About 3 hours, largely unattended

---

1 tablespoon vegetable or olive oil

1 whole beef brisket, about 5 pounds

Salt and lots of freshly ground pepper to taste

3 tablespoons butter (preferred) or more oil

2 cups minced onions

3 tablespoons tomato paste or 1 large ripe tomato, cored and chopped (peeled and seeded if you have time)

1 teaspoon minced garlic

3 cups chicken, beef, or vegetable stock, store-bought broth, or water

1 Preheat the oven to 325°F (you can also cook this brisket on top of the stove if you like). If you choose to brown the brisket first, heat a large casserole or Dutch oven that can later be covered over medium-high heat for 2 or 3 minutes. Add the oil, swirl it around, then add the beef. Sear it for about 5 minutes on each side, or until it is nicely browned. Season it with salt and pepper and remove to a platter.

2 Wipe out the pan with paper towels and return it to the stove; turn the heat to medium and add the butter. When it foams, add the onions and cook, stirring, until they are golden and soft, at least 10 minutes. Add salt and pepper, then stir in the tomato paste and the garlic. Return the meat to the pan, add the stock or water, and cover.

3 Cook over low heat or in the oven, turning the meat about every 30 minutes, until tender, 2½ to 3 hours. If the sauce seems too thin, allow the meat to rest on a platter for a few minutes while you boil the liquid down over high heat, scraping the bottom of the pan with a wooden spoon, until it thickens somewhat. Taste the sauce and add salt and/or pepper if needed. Slice the meat, return it to the sauce, and serve. Or let the meat sit in the sauce, over the lowest possible heat, for up to an hour before serving.

Ⓜ Spicy Beef Brisket Before searing, rub the meat all over with a mixture of 1 teaspoon salt, 2 teaspoons sugar, 2 teaspoons ground cumin, 1 teaspoon ground black pepper, $1/4$ teaspoon cayenne (more if you like), $1/2$ teaspoon ground coriander, and 2 teaspoons paprika. In Step 1, increase the oil to 2 tablespoons. In Step 2, use 2 tablespoons oil in place of the butter, and cook the onions over medium-high heat, stirring, until they begin to brown, about 10 minutes. Proceed as above.

Ⓜ Sweet Beef Brisket with Garlic Steps 1 and 2 remain unchanged. When the meat is somewhat tender but not quite done—after about $11/2$ to 2 hours of braising—add to the pot 1 pound peeled and chunked sweet potatoes; 2 carrots, peeled and chunked; $1/2$ cup dried apricots; $1/2$ cup dried pitted prunes (or other dried fruit); and 1 head of garlic, with most of the papery coating removed, cut in half horizontally. Continue to cook until all the fruits and vegetables are soft but not until they dissolve, 30 to 60 minutes. Serve, spreading the soft garlic on crusty bread.

Baked Ham with Maple Glaze

A good ham takes no work and—unless you have a house full of people—can be eaten for days. Most people like a sweet coating, which has little impact on the overall flavor but looks nice. Honestly—you can cook a good ham with nothing on it and it will still be delicious.

Makes 15 or more servings

Time: 1½ hours, largely unattended

---

1 (12- to 15-pound) cured ham

Cloves as needed

1 cup maple syrup (or use orange marmalade or apricot or peach preserves)

1 tablespoon Dijon mustard, or more to taste

2 cups or more dry apple cider or white wine (optional)

1 Preheat the oven to 350°F. Score the fatty layer of the ham in a diamond pattern and insert a clove into each diamond. Place the ham on a rack in a roasting pan.

2 Combine the maple syrup and mustard (if you're using marmalade, heat it gently to thin it out a bit). Spoon some of this mixture over the ham and bake for about 20 minutes. Baste again and continue to cook, basting once or twice with the pan juices, until the ham is hot, about an hour. If you want pan juices with which to top the ham (not necessary—it will be fine with no more than good mustard), add ½ cup of cider or wine to the bottom of the pan at the beginning of roasting and again if it threatens to become dry.

3 Remove the ham to a platter. To make pan juices, place the roasting pan on one or two burners over high heat. Add 1 cup of liquid to that already in the pan and cook, stirring and scraping, until the liquid has been reduced by about half and has thickened slightly. Carve the ham and serve with pan juices, mustard, or both.

Shopping Tip: Most supermarket hams, including canned hams, are just a step above the heavily processed ham you buy at the deli counter. For good-quality ham, mail order is usually your best bet; find a brand you like and stick to it. A good old-fashioned cure begins with a real brine of salt, water, and sugar, and concludes with a long period of smoking. A high-tech cure begins with a chemically augmented injected brine and ends with a douse of liquid smoke. You can taste the difference.

Crown Roast of Pork

Because this meat is fairly heavy, I prepare a light stuffing, using bread crumbs and fruit. I cook the stuffing separately to allow it to crisp and limit the amount of fat it absorbs, but you can place it in the center of the crown if you like. Order the roast a few days ahead.

Makes at least 10 or 12 servings

Time: About 2½ hours, largely unattended

½ cup dried apricots

1 crown roast of pork, 14 to 16 ribs, about 7 pounds

Salt and freshly ground black pepper to taste

1 carrot, peeled and chopped

1 celery stalk, chopped

1 onion, cut into quarters, plus 1 cup minced onion

3 tablespoons olive oil

1 tablespoon minced garlic

2 teaspoons minced fresh tarragon leaves or ½ teaspoon dried tarragon, crumbled

2 cups water or white wine, plus more as needed

½ pound (2 sticks) butter

4 cups plain bread crumbs, preferably fresh (page 37)

1 Preheat the oven to 450°F. Soak the apricots in hot water to cover. Sprinkle the roast with salt and pepper and place it on a rack in a roasting pan. Toss the carrot, celery, and quartered onion with 1 tablespoon of the olive oil and some salt and pepper; scatter them in the pan.

2 Mix the remaining olive oil together with half the garlic and tarragon. Rub the roast all over with this mixture.

3 Roast the meat for 20 minutes, then turn the heat down to 325°F. Moisten the vegetables with about ½ cup of liquid every 15 minutes.

4 In a deep skillet or saucepan over medium heat, melt the butter. Add the 1 cup minced onion and cook, stirring, until it is soft, about 5 minutes. Drain and chop the apricots and add them, then add the bread crumbs, remaining garlic and tarragon, salt, and pepper. Toss to combine. Put the stuffing in an 8-inch square or comparable baking dish in a 1- to 2-inch-thick layer and place in the oven. Cook the stuffing until it is crisp on top, then stir it up; repeat this process while you finish cooking the meat.

5 Cooking time for the roast will be about 2 hours; its internal temperature (check it in several places), should be about 150°F. When it's ready, remove it to a cutting board while you make the sauce. Lower the oven temperature to keep the stuffing warm (if it looks dry, baste it with juices from the roasting pan).

6 Pour or spoon off as much of the fat from the roasting pan as you can without losing the darker juices. Put the roasting pan on the stove over one or two burners set to medium-high. Add about 1½ cups of liquid and cook, stirring and scraping, until the liquid is reduced by about half. Remove the vegetables with a slotted spoon and press them into a strainer, adding any liquid you extract to the sauce.

7 Pile the stuffing into the center of the roast, then present the roast whole. Carve it, then serve with a bit of the stuffing, spooning a little of the sauce over it while passing the rest.

Roast Pork with Garlic and Rosemary

The basic roast pork. Serve with very light side dishes; this is the kind of dish that drives you wild and makes you eat more than you want to. If you want a more garlicky flavor, cut a clove of garlic into tiny slivers and, using a thin-bladed knife, insert them into the roast all over. The amount of liquid you need depends on how lean your roast is. You should able to make a sauce from the roast drippings, but have extra wine, broth, or water available if needed.

Makes 6 or more servings

Time: 1½ to 2 hours, largely unattended

Salt and freshly ground black pepper to taste

2 tablespoons minced fresh rosemary leaves or 1 teaspoon dried rosemary

¼ teaspoon cayenne (optional)

1 tablespoon sugar

1 teaspoon minced garlic

1 (3- to 4-pound) pork loin roast, bone-in, or 1 (2- to 3-pound) boneless pork roast, or a similar-size portion of fresh ham

About 2 cups dry white wine, or beef, chicken, or vegetable stock, or store-bought broth

1 tablespoon butter (optional)

1 Preheat the oven to 450°F. Mix a liberal amount of salt and pepper together with the rosemary, cayenne, sugar, and garlic, and rub it all over the roast. Place the meat in a roasting pan (use a rack if the roast is boneless, but don't bother if the bone is still in) and put in the oven. Roast, undisturbed, for 15 minutes.

2 Open the oven and pour about ½ cup of wine or stock over the roast; lower the heat to 325°F. Continue to roast, adding about ¼ cup of liquid every 15 minutes or so. If the liquid accumulates on the bottom of the pan, use it to baste; if not, add more.

3 Start checking the roast after 1¼ hours of total cooking time (it's likely to take about 1½ hours). When it is done—an instant-read thermometer will register 145° to 150°F—remove it to a warm platter. Put the roasting pan on the stove over one or two burners set to medium-high. If there is a great deal of liquid in it, reduce it to about ¾ cup, scraping the bottom of the pan with a wooden spoon to release any brown bits that have accumulated. If the pan is dry, add 1 cup of liquid and follow the same process. When the sauce has reduced some, stir in the butter if you like, slice the roast, and serve it with the sauce.

Grilled or Broiled Butterflied Leg of Lamb

Butterflied leg of lamb is often sold in supermarkets. (If you can only find bone-in leg, ask the butcher to remove it for you; it shouldn't take him more than 5 minutes.)

It's not cheap, but it's not outrageously expensive either, and leg of lamb qualifies as a true luxury because it is delicious, tender, and easy to cook. I think it's especially great because of its uneven thickness. This means if you cook the thickest parts to rare, you also get meat that is cooked to medium; and medium lamb, unlike medium beef, is moist and tender.

Makes at least 6 servings

Time: About 40 minutes, plus time to preheat the grill

---

1 (3- to 4-pound) butterflied leg of lamb

1 tablespoon olive oil

1 teaspoon minced garlic

1 tablespoon fresh rosemary leaves or 2 teaspoons dried rosemary

2 teaspoons fresh thyme leaves or 1 teaspoon dried thyme

Salt and freshly ground black pepper to taste

Minced fresh parsley leaves for garnish

Lemon wedges

1 Start a charcoal or wood fire or preheat a gas grill or broiler; the fire should be quite hot, and the rack should be at least 4 inches from the heat source. (Delay this step until you're just about ready to cook if you choose to marinate the meat.) Trim the lamb of any excess fat. Mix together the olive oil, garlic, rosemary, thyme, salt, and pepper; rub this mixture well into the lamb, making sure to get some into all the crevices. If you have the time, let the lamb sit, for an hour or more (refrigerate if it will be much longer).

2 Grill or broil the meat until it is nicely browned, even a little charred, on both sides, about 20 to 30 minutes, and the internal temperature at the thickest part is about 125°F; this will give you some lamb that is quite rare, as well as some that is nearly well done. Let rest for 5 minutes before slicing thinly, as you would a thick steak. Garnish, and serve with lemon wedges.

Preparation Tip: If you find or create a larger boneless leg—sometimes they are up to 6 pounds—either cut off a piece and freeze it for later use, or make the whole thing, but increase the other ingredients proportionally and plan to serve 8 to 12 people.

3 Ways to Flavor Leg of Lamb

1 Cumin mixed with honey and some minced orange peel

2 Minced ginger and scallions mixed with soy sauce

3 Your favorite curry powder, moistened with a bit of yogurt

Butterflied Leg of Lamb with Provençal Spices For the herbs in Step 1, substitute 1 teaspoon fresh or dried lavender, chopped; 1 teaspoon fresh or dried rosemary, chopped; 1/2 teaspoon fennel seeds. Proceed as in Steps 1 and 2, above.

Roast Rack of Lamb with Persillade

Not for formal occasions, but still impressive. When planning a meal with this dish, note that there are 7 ribs per rack, and only a couple of bites per rib, so you'll need 2 racks (or 14 ribs) for 4 people, although this could easily serve 5 people, and even 6 if there's plenty of other food and the crowd is not ravenous. (This is true despite the fact that many restaurants serve a whole rack per person—way too much for most eaters.)

Makes 4 servings

Time: 30 minutes

---

2 racks of lamb, about 2 pounds each

2 tablespoons olive oil

Salt and freshly ground black pepper to taste

1 cup plain bread crumbs, preferably fresh (page 37)

½ cup minced fresh parsley leaves

1 teaspoon minced garlic

1 Preheat the oven to 500°F. Trim the lamb of excess fat, but leave a layer of fat over the meat. Cut about halfway down the bones between the chops; this allows the meat between them to become crisp.

2 Combine all remaining ingredients and rub over the meat side of the racks. Put them in a roasting pan and place in the oven; roast for 20 minutes, and insert a meat thermometer straight in from one end into the meatiest part. If it reads 125°F or more, remove the lamb immediately. If it reads less, put the lamb back for 5 minutes, but no more. Remove and let sit for 5 minutes. Serve, separating the ribs by cutting down straight through them.

Shopping Tips: When buying rack of lamb, make sure it's not too large (2 pounds is the maximum) and ask the butcher to make sure the chine bone (backbone) is removed. This will allow you to easily cut through the ribs to separate them at the table.

Don't bother to ask to have the ribs "frenched" (the meat removed from the top of the bones); the crisp meat along the bones is one of the pleasures of a rack of lamb.

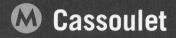
Here's a fairly basic cassoulet that is grand enough for any company; you can make it well in advance, then reheat it in the oven for about 30 minutes before adding the bread crumb–parsley mixture and browning.

Makes at least 12 servings

Time: 2½ hours, largely unattended

1½ pounds white beans (pea, navy, Great Northern, etc.)

Chicken, beef, or vegetable stock, store-bought broth, water, or a mixture, as needed

4 cloves garlic, crushed

1 medium-large onion, chopped

2 carrots, peeled and chopped

2 cups cored and chopped tomatoes (canned are fine; drain them first)

1 clove

3 or 4 sprigs fresh thyme, 1 teaspoon fresh thyme leaves, or ½ teaspoon dried thyme

2 bay leaves

¼ pound slab bacon or salt pork, in 1 piece

1 pound garlic (Italian) sausage

2 pounds pork shoulder

2 pounds boneless shoulder or leg of lamb, trimmed of excess fat

Salt and freshly ground black pepper to taste

1 cup red wine or water

1 tablespoon minced garlic

1½ cups plain bread crumbs (page 37)

1¼ cups minced fresh parsley leaves

1 Place the beans in a large Dutch oven or casserole with stock, broth, or water to cover. Turn the heat to high and bring to a boil; skim the foam if necessary. Turn the heat down so the beans simmer, then add the crushed garlic, onion, carrots, and tomatoes. Tie the clove, thyme, and bay leaves in a cheesecloth bag or place them in a tea ball, and cook along with the beans, stirring occasionally. In 1 hour or more, when the beans are tender but not mushy, turn off the heat.

2 As the beans are cooking, cook the bacon or salt pork in boiling water to cover for 2 minutes. Dice the meat and add it to the beans. Preheat the oven to 450°F.

3 Cut the garlic sausage, pork, and lamb into 1½-inch chunks. Place in a roasting pan and sprinkle liberally with salt and pepper. Roast, shaking the pan occasionally, until the meats are very well browned, about 30 minutes. Remove the meat and turn the oven to 350°F.

4 When the beans are tender and the meat is done, stir the meat into the beans, discarding the fat if you like. Turn the heat to medium-low and keep the mixture hot. Put the roasting pan over medium-high heat and add the wine or water; cook, stirring and scraping to loosen any brown bits that have stuck to the bottom of the pan, then add this liquid to the stew. (The recipe can be prepared a day or two in advance up to this point; cool, place in a covered container, and refrigerate.)

5 Taste the stew for salt and pepper and add some if necessary. Stir in the garlic. Combine the bread crumbs and 1 cup of the parsley and spread this mixture over the stew. Bake for 15 to 20 minutes, or until the bread crumbs have browned nicely. Garnish with the remaining parsley and serve.

Shopping Tip: If you can find duck confit (preserved duck)—it's sold in some specialty markets—it makes a super addition here. Crisp it up in a skillet and add it at the last minute, or simmer it along with the rest of the meat. A piece of duck breast, seared just before serving, also makes the cassoulet more special.

6 | Side Dishes

 Make Ahead

Asparagus with Parmesan

A simple but special side dish that people really love. Butter and Parmesan are always a great combination. If you don't want to use butter, just eliminate it; the cheese alone will flavor the asparagus nicely.

Makes 4 servings

Time: 30 minutes

1½ to 2 pounds asparagus, bottom ends snapped off, peeled up to the beginning of the flower (very thin asparagus need no peeling)

2 to 4 tablespoons butter, plus some for greasing the pan

Salt and freshly ground black pepper to taste

About 1 cup freshly grated Parmesan cheese

1 Simmer, steam, or microwave the asparagus; undercook it a little bit.

To simmer, lay them down in a skillet that can hold the spears without crowding; cover with salted water; cover the skillet; and turn the heat to high. Cook just until the thick part of the stalks can be pierced with a knife.

To steam, stand them up in a pot with an inch of salted water on the bottom (it's nice, but hardly essential, to tie them in a bundle first). Cover and turn the heat to high. Cook just until the thick part of the stalks can be pierced with a knife.

To microwave, lay them in a microwave-proof plate or shallow bowl with about 2 tablespoons of salted water; cover with a lid or plastic wrap. Microwave on high for 3 minutes, shake the container, and continue to microwave at 1-minute intervals, just until the thick part of the stalks can be pierced with a knife.

2 Drain and plunge the asparagus into ice water, then drain and dry. (You may prepare the recipe in advance up to this point; refrigerate, well wrapped or in a covered container, for up to 2 days before proceeding.) Preheat the oven to 450°F.

3 Butter a casserole or baking pan, then place the asparagus in it. Dot with as much or as little butter as you like and sprinkle with salt and pepper. Scatter about two-thirds of the cheese over the asparagus and bake until the cheese is just beginning to turn light brown, 10 to 15 minutes. Sprinkle with the remaining Parmesan and serve.

Brussels Sprouts with Bacon

Brussels sprouts look like miniature cabbages, and that's what they are. Like cabbage, they must not be overcooked, or they become soggy and strong-flavored. But bought well and handled simply, they can be wonderful; bacon finishes them off nicely, but this recipe is great without it, too.

Simmering is the easiest way to cook Brussels sprouts. Steaming and microwaving are also fine, but you must keep a close watch on them to avoid overcooking.

Makes 4 servings

Time: 20 minutes

---

1 to 1½ pounds Brussels sprouts, trimmed (at right)

2 tablespoons butter or extra-virgin olive oil

1 clove garlic, smashed (optional)

1 tablespoon plain bread crumbs

1 tablespoon freshly squeezed lemon juice

1 tablespoon minced fresh parsley leaves

Salt and freshly ground black pepper to taste

¼ cup crumbled cooked bacon (optional)

1 Bring a large pot of water to the boil; salt it. Add the Brussels sprouts and, keeping the heat high, boil them just until tender (check with a thin-bladed knife), about 10 minutes; do not overcook. Drain and refresh in cold water. (You may prepare the recipe in advance up to this point; refrigerate, well wrapped or in a covered container, for up to 2 days before proceeding.)

2 Place the butter or oil in a large, deep skillet over medium heat; add the garlic. When the butter foam subsides or the oil is hot, add the sprouts and the bread crumbs. Stir until hot, about 3 minutes.

3 Remove the garlic, toss the sprouts with the lemon juice and parsley, and season to taste. Sprinkle with the bacon, toss, and serve.

Shopping Tip: With Brussels sprouts, the smaller the better is a good rule. Reject any with yellow leaves, loose leaves, or those that are soft or not tightly packed. Generally, they are a winter vegetable, found from September or October through early spring.

Preparation Tip: Remove the Brussels sprouts stem and any loose leaves. Some people suggest cutting an "x" in the root bottom to ensure even cooking, but I haven't found that it matters much.

Pureed Butternut Squash with Ginger

Because it is so porous, winter squash absorbs water readily; thus it's better to cook it above water rather than in it.

Makes 4 servings

Time: About 20 minutes

1½ pounds butternut or other winter squash, peeled and cut into chunks

2 tablespoons butter

1 to 2 teaspoons peeled and roughly chopped fresh ginger or 1 teaspoon ground ginger, or to taste

Salt and freshly ground black pepper to taste

1 teaspoon brown sugar, or to taste (optional)

1 Place the squash in a steamer above about 1 inch of salted water. Cover and cook until the squash is very tender, about 20 minutes. To microwave, place the squash and 2 tablespoons of water in a microwave-proof plate or shallow bowl; cover with a lid or plastic wrap. Microwave on high for 3 minutes, shake the container, and continue to microwave at 2-minute intervals, until the squash is very tender.

2 While it is still hot, place the squash in the container of a food processor with the butter and ginger; process until smooth. Taste and add salt, pepper, and brown sugar if you like. (You may prepare the recipe in advance up to this point; refrigerate, well wrapped or in a covered container, for up to 2 days before proceeding.)

3 Reheat over low heat or in a microwave and serve.

Preparation Tip: Peel butternut squash with a paring knife; its skin is too tough for a vegetable peeler (and be ruthless, rather than careful; squash is cheap). The densest, best "meat" is in the narrow part, where there are no seeds, so use that part first.

4 Flavorings for Pureed Squash

Try any of the following, alone or in combination:

1 A small handful of fresh herbs, including parsley, cilantro, mint, and sage

2 Maple syrup or honey in place of brown sugar

3 Olive oil in place of butter

4 Other ground spices in place of ginger, including cardamom, cinnamon, mace, and nutmeg

Boiled, Grilled, or Roasted Chestnuts

Chestnuts are cooked much like vegetables, so I have included them here. Boil chestnuts only if you are going to use them in another recipe, like stuffing, afterward. For eating chestnuts out of hand, roast them in the oven or grill them over hot coals.

Makes 1 pound, 4 to 6 servings

Time: About 30 minutes, plus time to preheat the grill

1 pound chestnuts, flat side cut
(see below)

1   To boil: Place in a pot with lightly salted water to cover and bring to a boil. Turn off the heat after 3 or 4 minutes. Remove a few chestnuts from the water at a time and use a sharp knife to cut off the outer and inner skins.

2   To grill or roast: Start a charcoal or wood fire, or preheat a gas grill, or turn the oven to 450°F. Place the chestnuts directly on the grill, or on a sheet of aluminum foil with holes poked in it, or on a baking sheet. Grill (preferably with the cover down) or roast, turning occasionally, until you can remove the shells easily, about 15 minutes. Eat warm, out of hand.

Shopping Tip: In much of Europe, chestnuts fall to the ground through September and October, so the best season is definitely autumn. Buy heavy, big, full, unblemished nuts; they dry out as they age, and begin to rattle around in their shells. Their shelf life is not as long as you might think—just a week or two; refrigeration is neither necessary nor helpful.

Cooking Tip: Cooked, shelled, and skinned chestnuts are good mashed with butter, just like potatoes, or braised with other vegetables or meats, or gently sautéed.

Preparing Chestnuts

Before cooking a chestnut, score the flat side with a sharp knife, making an "x."

After cooking, remove both outer shell and inner skin.

Slow-Cooked Green Beans

Although "overcooking" vegetables is out of favor, these are meltingly tender and delicious. They are a simple but wonderful addition to any holiday meal.

Makes 4 servings

Time: About 1 hour

About 1½ pounds green beans, the smaller the better, washed and trimmed

¼ cup extra-virgin olive oil, plus more for sprinkling

1 cup minced onion

1 cup cored, peeled, seeded, and chopped tomatoes (canned are fine; drain them first)

½ cup water, plus more if needed

Salt and freshly ground black pepper to taste

Freshly squeezed lemon juice to taste, plus a few drops for sprinkling

1 Combine all ingredients in a large saucepan and bring to a boil. Cover tightly and cook over medium-low heat for 1 hour, checking every 15 minutes and adding a few tablespoons of water if necessary. Longer cooking, up to 1 hour longer, will not hurt a bit.

2 When the beans are very tender and all the liquid is absorbed, they are ready. (You may prepare the recipe in advance up to this point; refrigerate, well wrapped or in a covered container, for up to 2 days before proceeding.) Serve hot or at room temperature, sprinkled with a little more oil and a few more drops of lemon juice.

Shopping Tips: You can choose any of a number of green beans: the thin haricot vert (common in France), the yard-long bean (originally from China, now grown here also), the wax or yellow bean (obviously not green at all), and the romano, a gardening favorite. All can be eaten raw, briefly cooked—so that they remain crunchy—or cooked to complete tenderness.

Sold year-round, green beans are at their best in summer, when they're most likely to be local. Buy beans that snap rather than fold when you bend them in half, and avoid any with browning or other obvious signs of spoilage.

Preparation Tip: Store green beans, loosely wrapped in plastic, in the vegetable bin, and use as soon as possible, preferably within a day.

Potato Pancakes

These are the traditional latkes, served in many Jewish households during Hanukkah. They are excellent with any meat served with gravy, sour cream, or with applesauce (see the recipe below to make it yourself).

Makes 6 servings

Time: About 40 minutes

About 2 pounds baking potatoes, such as Idaho or Russet, peeled

1 medium onion

2 eggs

Salt and freshly ground black pepper to taste

2 tablespoons plain bread crumbs or matzo meal

Canola or other neutral oil as needed

1 Grate the potatoes by hand or with the grating disk of a food processor. Drain in a strainer; grate the onion. Preheat the oven to 200°F.

2 In a large bowl, beat the eggs with the salt, pepper, and bread crumbs or matzo meal; stir in the potatoes and onion.

3 Place a ⅛-inch layer of oil in a large, deep skillet and turn the heat to medium. When the oil is hot, drop the potato batter into it by the ¼ cup or large spoon. Cook until browned on both sides, about 10 minutes per pancake. Drain pancakes on paper towels and keep warm in the oven until all of them are finished. Serve hot, with sour cream or applesauce.

Shopping Tip: Baking potatoes (Idaho or Russet) are best for potato pancakes, because they're high in starch, so they will bind better. All-purpose potatoes like Yukon Gold do a decent job as well. If you're stuck with low starch potatoes ("new," whether red or white), add an extra egg and a little more bread crumbs.

Preparation Tips: For different latkes, you can substitute grated sweet potatoes (or, for that matter, carrots) for about one-third of the white potatoes—no more, or the mixture will not be sufficiently starchy.

You can make your own applesauce by cooking a few pounds of apples, cut in half (if you have a food mill, you need not peel and core them, but otherwise you must), with about 1/2-inch of water in a covered pot. Turn the heat to medium-high. When the mixture bubbles, uncover and turn it to low. Cook, stirring occasionally, until the apples break down, about 30 minutes. Let cool, then add sugar if necessary. Put through a food mill, discarding the solids that remain.

Crispy Sautéed Potatoes with Rosemary

This is a simple way to get deliciously crisp and flavorful potatoes, and everyone loves them no matter how simple they are compared to the rest of the meal.

Makes 4 servings

Time: 45 minutes

1½ to 2 pounds waxy red or white potatoes, peeled and cut into ½-inch to 1-inch cubes

¼ cup olive oil, more or less

2 teaspoons chopped fresh rosemary leaves or ½ teaspoon dried rosemary

1 teaspoon minced garlic

Salt and freshly ground black pepper to taste

1 Place the potatoes in a pot of salted water, bring to a boil, and simmer until nearly tender, 10 to 15 minutes. Drain well.

2 Heat the oil over medium-high heat in a 12-inch non-stick skillet for 3 or 4 minutes. You can use more oil (for crisper potatoes) or less (for less fat). Add the potatoes and cook, tossing and stirring from time to time (not constantly), until they are nicely browned all over, 10 to 20 minutes. Add the rosemary and garlic, salt, and pepper, and continue to cook for 5 more minutes, stirring frequently. Adjust seasoning and serve.

Baked Sweet Potatoes

You must bake sweet potatoes in a baking pan, because they tend to drip their syrupy juice, which clings to everything. Line the pan with aluminum foil to ease cleanup.

Makes 4 servings

Time: About 1 hour

---

4 sweet potatoes

Butter

1 Preheat the oven to 425°F. Line a baking pan with aluminum foil and place the potatoes in it.

2 Pierce each of the potatoes a few times with a skewer or thin-bladed knife. Bake, shaking the pan once or twice, for about 1 hour, or until the potatoes are very soft and tender. Serve with butter.

Shopping Tip: Sweet potatoes are the familiar bright orange-fleshed tubers (more exotic varieties have rose, purple, yellow, or white flesh) of fall and winter. They are not yams, which—popular nomenclature to the contrary—are a different tuber.

Cooking Tip: Brilliant baked, sweet potatoes are also good handled in many of the same ways you would treat white potatoes and winter squash—fried, mashed, or roasted.

Baked Sweet Potatoes with Corn Scoop the meat out from its skin and combine with cooked corn kernels, about 2 tablespoons per potato; butter, about 1 tablespoon per potato; and salt, pepper, and brown sugar (not too much) to taste. Reheat gently in a non-stick skillet.

 Creamed Spinach

One of the most festive of vegetable dishes, one of the most popular, and one of the easiest to make. You can triple or quadruple this recipe easily.

   If you want to make a simpler, lower-fat version, simply proceed with Step 1, then sprinkle the spinach with a little lemon juice and olive oil and serve. The same technique can be used with kale, collards, chard, or other greens; just vary the cooking time as necessary to make sure the greens are cooked until tender.

Makes 4 servings

Time: About 20 minutes

---

1 pound spinach, trimmed and washed (or use one 10-ounce package frozen spinach)

¾ cup cream

1 tablespoon butter

Freshly grated nutmeg to taste (just a little)

Salt and freshly ground black pepper to taste

1 Any of these can be done in advance: To boil the spinach, bring a large pot of water to a boil; salt it. Place the spinach in the water and cook for about 1 minute, or until it is bright green and tender. To steam the spinach, place it in covered saucepan with about a tablespoon of water (or with the water that clings to its leaves after washing). Cook about 4 minutes, until the spinach is bright green and tender. To microwave the spinach, place in a microwave-proof plate or shallow bowl with just the water that clings to its leaves after washing; add salt and cover with a lid or plastic wrap. Microwave on high for 1 minute, shake the container, and continue to microwave at 1-minute intervals, just until it wilts.

2 Cool the cooked spinach; squeeze excess moisture from it and chop it. Place the cream in a large saucepan, turn the heat to medium-high, and bring just about to a boil. Turn the heat to low and add the spinach, butter, nutmeg, salt, and pepper. Simmer, stirring occasionally, until the mixture is creamy and very soft, about 10 minutes. Serve hot or refrigerate, covered, for a day or two; reheat before serving.

Shopping Tip: Fresh spinach leaves must be plump; any wilting or yellowing is a bad sign. Store it, loosely wrapped in plastic, in the vegetable bin, but use it as fast as you can. It will keep for a few days. Sold year-round, in season locally in cool but not cold or hot weather. Wash it well, in several changes of water; it's sandy. Remove the thickest stems, but leave thinner ones on; they'll be fine.

Traditional Cranberry Sauce

Most cranberry sauce is too sweet, but that's traditional, and it has this advantage: The sauce will gel upon cooling. If you want to make a less-sweet sauce, by all means do, but expect it to be runnier. If you want a very firm sauce, make the variation.

Makes about 1 quart

Time: 20 minutes, plus time to chill

---

4 cups (about 1 pound) fresh cranberries, picked over and washed, or frozen cranberries

1½ cups sugar

2 cups water

1 Combine all ingredients in a medium saucepan and turn the heat to medium-low. Cover and cook, stirring occasionally, until the berries are broken, 10 to 15 minutes.

2 Transfer to a bowl; cool, then chill until ready to serve. This keeps well, refrigerated, for up to a week.

Shopping Tip: Cranberries should be firm and whole; you can freeze them almost indefinitely, or store them in the refrigerator for weeks. Incredibly, it doesn't make much difference.

Firm Cranberry Sauce or Cranberry Jelly Increase sugar to 2 cups. For Firm Cranberry Sauce, proceed as above. For jelly, cook 5 minutes longer, stirring frequently. Pass through a sieve into a mold, bowl, or jelly jars and cool, then chill until firm. Slice to serve.

Rice Pilaf

There are many definitions of pilaf, but two are common to all: The rice must be briefly cooked in oil or butter before adding liquid, and the liquid must be flavorful. The oil or butter may be flavored with vegetables, herbs, or spices; the liquid may be anything from lobster stock to yogurt; and other foods may be added to the pot.

Makes 4 servings

Time: About 30 minutes

2 tablespoons butter or oil

1 cup chopped onion

1½ cups long-grain rice

Salt and freshly ground black pepper

2½ cups chicken, beef, vegetable stock, store-bought broth, or water, heated to the boiling point

Minced fresh parsley leaves for garnish

1   Place the butter or oil in a large, deep skillet that can later be covered and turn the heat to medium-high. When the butter melts or the oil is hot, add the onion. Cook, stirring, until the onion softens but does not begin to brown, 5 to 8 minutes.

2   Add the rice all at once, turn the heat to medium, and stir until the rice is glossy and completely coated with oil or butter, 2 or 3 minutes. Season well, then turn the heat down to low and add the liquid, all at once. Cover the pan.

3   Cook for 15 minutes, then check the rice. When the rice is tender and the liquid is absorbed, it's done. If not, cook for 2 or 3 minutes and check again. Check the seasoning, garnish, and serve immediately.

Wild Rice

Wild rice is indigenous to North America and, though technically a grass, it is treated as a grain. There is cultivated wild rice (mostly from California) and wild wild rice (mostly from Minnesota); either can be quite good. It is expensive—usually upward of $10 a pound—and so it is often combined with white rice (see the variation).

Makes 4 servings

Time: About 40 minutes

1 cup wild rice, well rinsed

2 cups chicken, beef, or vegetable stock, store-bought broth, or water

1 bay leaf

Salt and freshly ground black pepper to taste

1 tablespoon butter (optional)

Minced fresh parsley leaves for garnish

1 Combine all ingredients except the butter and parsley in a medium saucepan and bring to a boil over medium-high heat.

2 Cover, turn the heat to low, and cook, undisturbed, for 30 minutes. Check the progress: The rice is done when the grains have puffed up and are quite tender, regardless of whether the liquid has been absorbed. If the rice is not done, continue to cook, adding more liquid if necessary. If it is done, drain if necessary.

3 Stir in the optional butter, garnish, and serve.

Shopping Tip: If you can, avoid the little boxes of wild rice you find in the supermarket; the price is outrageous, and the quality suspect. Look for a good mail order source (you might start with www.zingermans.com).

Wild Rice with Curried Nuts While the rice is cooking in the above recipe, melt 2 tablespoons butter in a large skillet. Add 1 tablespoon curry powder and cook, stirring, for 1 minute. Stir in 1/2 to 1 cup broken-up cashews, almonds, pecans, or walnuts (broken into bits, not finely chopped). Cook, stirring, until they begin to brown. Turn off the heat until the rice is done, then drain the rice if necessary and add it to the nut-butter mixture. Cook over medium-low heat, stirring, until hot.

Wild Rice with White Rice Start with equal parts of cooked wild and white rice. Cook as for Rice Pilaf (page 76).

Southern Beans and Rice

Bacon, peas, and rice—southern staples—comprise Hoppin' John, our best indigenous rice and bean dish, often served at year-end celebrations to bring good luck in the new year.

Makes 4 to 6 servings

Time: 1½ to 2 hours, largely unattended

1 cup black-eyed or other dried peas, washed and picked over

¼ pound slab bacon or 1 smoked ham hock

1 large onion, chopped

1 (4-inch) sprig fresh rosemary, 2 sprigs fresh thyme, or ½ teaspoon dried rosemary or thyme

Salt and freshly ground black pepper to taste

1½ cups long-grain rice

1 Place the peas in a medium pot with the bacon or ham hock, onion, herb, and water to cover by at least 2 inches. Bring to a boil over medium-high heat.

2 Turn the heat down to medium and cook, skimming any foam that arises, until the peas are tender, 1 to 1½ hours. Remove the meat and reduce the liquid to about 3 cups; as the liquid is reducing, cut the meat into chunks, removing extremely fatty pieces if you like. Return it to the pot.

3 Taste the cooking liquid and add salt and more pepper if needed. Remove the rosemary or thyme sprigs, if used. Stir in the rice and cook, covered, until the rice is done and the liquid is absorbed, 15 to 20 minutes. This can sit for 15 to 20 minutes before serving.

Shopping Tip: Both slab bacon and smoked ham hocks are sold in most supermarkets (those without additives are best).

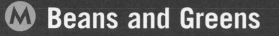

Beans and Greens

Best with white beans, whether small or large. Cook them until they are just about falling apart; these should be very creamy. These can be made ahead and stored, covered, in the refrigerator for a day or two. Serve at room temperature or reheat.

Makes 4 servings

Time: 1 to 2 hours, largely unattended

½ pound dried white beans, washed and picked over

1 medium onion, unpeeled

1 bay leaf

1 clove

Salt and freshly ground black pepper to taste

1½ pounds dark greens, such as kale, collards, mustard, or broccoli raab, well washed and roughly chopped

1 tablespoon minced garlic

4 teaspoons extra-virgin olive oil

1 Place the beans in a large pot with water to cover. Turn the heat to high and bring to a boil.

2 Cut a slit in the onion and insert the bay leaf; insert the clove into the onion as well and put the onion in the pot. Turn the heat down so the beans simmer. Cover loosely.

3 When the beans begin to soften, after about 30 minutes, season with salt and pepper. Continue to cook, stirring occasionally, until the beans are tender but still intact, about 1 hour; add additional water if necessary.

4 Add the greens to the pot and continue to cook until they are tender, 10 to 30 minutes, depending on the thickness of the stems. If you want a soupy mixture, add more water.

5 Remove the onion. Season the stew with additional salt and pepper. About 3 minutes before serving, add the garlic and stir. Spoon the beans and greens into individual bowls and drizzle with olive oil (or see the variation, below).

Beans and Greens Gratin Cook as above. When you're done, stir in 1 tablespoon olive oil and spread the mixture in a lightly oiled baking dish. Preheat the broiler. Top the mixture with 1 cup bread crumbs (preferably fresh, page 37). Drizzle with more olive oil to taste. Run under the broiler, about 4 to 6 inches from the heat source, until lightly browned, about 5 minutes. Serve hot or at room temperature.

ⓂMy Favorite Bread Stuffing

I tend to be pretty conservative with almost all aspects of turkey-making for feasts, and that includes the stuffing. I keep it simple and strive to make it one of the less challenging aspects of the meal. As you already know, any stuffing you make from scratch is going to be infinitely better than the instant kind most people are used to, so you're way ahead of the game.

   Like almost everyone else, I have cut back on my use of butter in recent years. But this classic dressing, which is based on a wonderful recipe by James Beard, is so great that I refuse to compromise when I make it. Check out the variations if you prefer to use olive oil.

   You can use this stuffing for any bird, or as a side dish year-round.

Makes about 6 cups, enough for
a 12-pound bird

Time: 20 minutes, plus baking time

½ pound (2 sticks) butter

1 cup minced onion

½ cup pine nuts or chopped walnuts

6 to 8 cups fresh bread crumbs
(page 37)

1 tablespoon minced fresh tarragon
or sage leaves or 1 teaspoon dried
crumbled tarragon or sage

Salt and freshly ground black pepper
to taste

½ cup minced scallions

½ cup minced fresh parsley leaves

1 Melt the butter over medium heat in a large, deep skillet, Dutch oven, or casserole. Add the onion and cook, stirring, until it softens, about 5 minutes. Add the nuts and cook, stirring almost constantly, until they begin to brown, about 3 minutes.

2 Add the bread crumbs and the tarragon or sage and toss to mix. Turn the heat to low. Add the salt, pepper, and scallions. Toss again; taste and adjust seasoning if necessary. Add the parsley and stir. Turn off the heat. (You may prepare the recipe in advance up to this point; refrigerate, well wrapped or in a covered container, for up to a day before proceeding.)

3 Pack this into the turkey if you like, or simply put it in an ovenproof glass or enameled casserole and bake it with the turkey during the last 45 minutes of cooking.

Preparation Tips: If you want a moist, soft, juicy stuffing, pack it in the bird. But if you want a clean-flavored, crisp stuffing that can stand on its own as a side dish, consider cooking it on its own. (And, although this is not really a concern if you cook your birds thoroughly—the temperature of the stuffing needs to reach 165°F, just like the meat—the chances of harmful bacteria developing in the bird are greater if you cook the stuffing inside of it.)

Don't skimp on the fat or the seasonings. Lean, underseasoned stuffing is little more than mushy bread.

ⓜ Bread Stuffing with Sage and Chestnuts Start by boiling or roasting 3/4 to 1 pound chestnuts until they are tender (see Boiled, Grilled, or Roasted Chestnuts, page 69). Shell, skin, and chop. Cook the onions as in Step 1, above. When they are soft, add the chestnuts and 1/2 cup dry white wine (omit nuts). Simmer for 5 minutes. In Step 2, use sage and just 2 tablespoons minced fresh parsley; proceed as above.

ⓜ Bread Stuffing with Sausage In Step 1, omit butter. Cook 1 pound sausage meat (you can squeeze the meat from links) in its own fat over medium heat until pinkish-gray. Spoon off the fat, then add the onion and cook until the onion softens, about 5 minutes. Omit the nuts. Add 1 tablespoon minced garlic, 1 teaspoon peeled and minced fresh ginger (or 1/2 teaspoon ground ginger), and 1 teaspoon ground cumin (optional). Omit tarragon or sage; proceed with Step 2.

ⓜ Bread Stuffing with Mushrooms In Step 1, use butter or olive oil and cook 1 cup trimmed and sliced white mushrooms along with the onion. If you have them, add 1 ounce soaked, drained, trimmed, and minced porcini mushrooms at the same time. Add 1 teaspoon minced garlic when the mushrooms have softened. Omit the nuts. Use sage or thyme (1 teaspoon fresh or 1/2 teaspoon dried) and proceed with Step 2.

7 | Breads, Pies, Cookies, Cakes

Ⓜ Make Ahead

Serving homemade bread means you made a special effort, even though it is really quite simple to make; just set aside enough time. These rich, buttery rolls won't fail to impress.

Makes about 20 rolls

Time: At least 2½ hours, largely unattended

3½ cups (about 1 pound) all-purpose flour, plus more as needed

1 tablespoon salt

1 tablespoon sugar

2 teaspoons instant yeast

3 tablespoons cold butter, plus a little soft butter for greasing the bowl

1 egg, plus second egg for brushing on rolls if desired

1 cup milk, plus more as needed

Making Rolls

To make dinner rolls, first roll a small lump of dough on a lightly floured surface until the seam is closed and smooth.

Slash it with a sharp knife or razor before cooking.

1 Combine the flour, salt, sugar, and yeast in the container of a food processor fitted with the steel blade and process for 5 seconds. Add the cold butter and 1 egg and process for 10 seconds. With the machine running, pour (don't drizzle) the milk through the feed tube. Process about 30 seconds, then remove the cover. The dough should be in a well-defined, barely sticky, easy-to-handle ball. If it is too dry, add milk 1 tablespoon at a time and process for 5 or 10 seconds after each addition. If it is too wet, which is unlikely, add another tablespoon or two of flour and process briefly. Knead for 1 minute or so by hand. It should be smooth, silky, and very elastic, and not too stiff.

2 Grease a large bowl, shape the dough into a rough ball, place it in the bowl, and cover with plastic wrap or a damp towel. Let rise for 1 to 1½ hours, until nearly doubled in bulk. Deflate the ball and shape it once again into a ball; let rest on a lightly floured surface for about 15 minutes, covered.

3 Roll the dough out until it is about ½ inch thick, using no more flour than necessary to keep the dough from sticking to the work surface or rolling pin. Use a 2-inch cookie cutter or other utensil to cut out circles, or simply pinch off bits of dough and shape them into round balls (see illustrations, at left).

4 Preheat the oven to 375°F. If you want the rolls to have a glossy top, brush them lightly with an egg beaten with a little milk. Bake about 20 minutes, or until the rolls are lightly browned and their bottoms sound hollow when tapped. Cool on a rack, or serve straight from the oven.

Cranberry Nut Bread

Sweet, tart, and rich, this is not only the model bread for Thanksgiving or Christmas, it's the perfect quick bread for afternoon tea, brunches, and picnics. The added orange is a great flavor boost.

Makes 1 loaf

Time: About 1¼ hours

---

4 tablespoons (½ stick) cold butter, plus some for greasing the pan

2 cups (about 9 ounces) all-purpose flour

1 cup sugar

1½ teaspoons baking powder

½ teaspoon baking soda

1 teaspoon salt

¾ cup orange juice

1 tablespoon minced or grated orange zest

1 egg

1 cup cranberries, washed, dried, and coarsely chopped

½ cup chopped walnuts or pecans

1   Preheat the oven to 350°F. Grease a 9 × 5-inch bread pan.

2   Stir together the dry ingredients. Cut the butter into bits, then use a fork or two knives to cut it into the dry ingredients, until there are no pieces bigger than a small pea. (You can use a food processor for this step, which makes it quite easy, but you should not use a food processor for the remaining steps or the bread will be tough.)

3   Beat together the orange juice, zest, and egg. Pour into the dry ingredients, mixing just enough to moisten; do not beat, and do not mix until the batter is smooth.

4   Fold in the cranberries and the nuts, then pour and spoon the batter into the loaf pan. Bake about an hour, or until the bread is golden brown and a toothpick inserted into its center comes out clean. Cool on a rack for 15 minutes before removing from the pan.

ⓜ Traditional Apple Pie

Nothing says American holiday meal like apple pie. There are countless ways of making a "perfect" apple pie, but this recipe is a great place to start. Once you have the essentials down, you can improvise with spices and toppings.

I usually don't thicken the filling for a simple apple pie, but if you want to make sure the juices don't run, add 1½ tablespoons cornstarch or 2 tablespoons instant tapioca when you toss the apples with the spices. I also keep spices to a minimum, since I'd rather taste the apples; you could safely double their quantity if you like a spicy pie, and add a pinch of allspice and/or cloves if you like.

Makes about 8 servings

Time: About 1½ hours, plus cooling time

¼ cup brown sugar

¼ cup white sugar, or more if you would like a very sweet pie, plus a little for the top of the pie

½ teaspoon ground cinnamon

⅛ teaspoon freshly grated nutmeg

Pinch salt

5 or 6 Cortland, McIntosh, or other good cooking apples

1 tablespoon freshly squeezed lemon juice

1½ tablespoons cornstarch or 2 tablespoons instant tapioca (optional)

1 recipe Pie Shell for a Two-Crust Pie (page 89), bottom crust fitted into a 9-inch pie pan, top crust transferred to a rimless baking sheet, both refrigerated

2 tablespoons unsalted butter, cut into bits

Milk as needed

1   Toss together the sugars, spices, and salt. Peel and core the apples and cut them into ½- to ¾-inch-thick slices. Toss the apples and lemon juice with the dry ingredients, adding the cornstarch or tapioca if you want a less runny pie.

2   Pile the apples into the rolled-out bottom crust, making the pile a little higher in the center than at the sides. Dot with butter. Carefully transfer the top crust from the baking sheet to the pie plate, covering the filling and pressing the edges together with those of the bottom crust to form a seal. Trim if necessary, and decorate the edges with a fork or your fingers, using any of the methods illustrated on page 89. Refrigerate while you preheat the oven to 450°F.

3   Place the pie on a cookie sheet and brush the top lightly with milk; sprinkle with sugar. Use a sharp paring knife to cut two or three 2-inch-long vent holes in the top crust; this will allow steam to escape. Place in the oven and bake for 10 minutes. Reduce the heat to 350°F and bake another 40 to 50 minutes, or until the pie is golden brown. Do not underbake. Cool on a rack before serving warm or at room temperature.

Apple-Pear Pie Add 1 tablespoon peeled and minced fresh ginger or 1 teaspoon ground ginger to the mixture of dry ingredients. Use half apples and half pears. Add 2 tablespoons cornstarch or 3 tablespoons instant tapioca to the mixture if you want a less runny pie.

Dutch Apple Pie Add 2 tablespoons cornstarch or 3 tablespoons instant tapioca to the mixture. Proceed as above, making sure to cut a large vent hole in the center of the top crust. About 30 minutes into the baking time, pour $1/2$ cup heavy cream into the vent hole and finish baking as above.

Deep-Dish Apple Pie with Streusel Topping Use a Generous Pie Shell for a 10-Inch or Larger Pie, or Deep-Dish Pie (page 89). Increase all filling ingredients by one-third. Fill the pie as above. Cream together (you can use the food processor for this) 8 tablespoons (1 stick) butter and $1/2$ cup brown sugar. Stir in $1/2$ cup chopped walnuts or pecans, 1 tablespoon freshly squeezed lemon juice, $1/2$ teaspoon ground cinnamon (or to taste) and just enough flour to make the mixture crumbly, $1/2$ cup or less. Strew this mixture over the top of the apples. Bake at 375°F for 45 to 60 minutes, or until the center of the pie is bubbly and the streusel mixture and bottom crust are nicely browned.

5 Easy Additions to Apple Pie

1 Chopped nuts, $1/2$ to 1 cup

2 Any appealing spice, generally in small amounts, such as minced fresh or crystallized ginger, allspice, or cloves

3 Bourbon or rum sprinkled over the top just before baking, about 2 tablespoons

4 Cranberries, left whole, about 1 cup (increase the amount of sugar slightly)

5 Dried fruit, such as raisins or dried cranberries, $1/2$ to 1 cup

Ⓜ Flaky Pie Crust

I like to add a little sugar to any pie shell that will contain a sweet filling, which essentially means any dessert pie shell. Many crusts are bland and tasteless, and sugar changes that. In addition, it aids in browning. I also add a scant amount of flour initially, which gives you the leeway to add flour liberally during rolling.

For any single-crust pie, 8 to 10 inches in diameter

Time: About 45 minutes, including resting time

1⅛ cups (about 5 ounces) all-purpose flour, plus some for dusting work surface

½ teaspoon salt

1 teaspoon sugar

8 tablespoons (1 stick) cold unsalted butter, cut into about 8 pieces

About 3 tablespoons ice water, plus more if necessary

1   Combine the flour, salt, and sugar in the container of a food processor; pulse once or twice. Add the butter and turn on the machine; process until the butter and flour are blended and the mixture looks like cornmeal, about 10 seconds.

2   Place the mixture in a bowl and sprinkle 3 tablespoons of water over it. Use a wooden spoon or a rubber spatula to gradually gather the mixture into a ball; if the mixture seems dry, add another ½ tablespoon ice water. When you can make the mixture into a ball with your hands, do so. Wrap in plastic, flatten into a small disk, and freeze the dough for 10 minutes (or refrigerate for 30 minutes); this will ease rolling. (You can also refrigerate the dough for a day or two, or freeze it almost indefinitely.)

3   You can roll the dough between two sheets of plastic wrap, usually quite successfully; sprinkle both sides of it with a little more flour, then proceed. Or sprinkle a countertop or large board with flour. Unwrap the dough and place it on the work surface; sprinkle its top with flour. If the dough is hard, let it rest for a few minutes; it should give a little when you press your fingers into it.

4   Roll with light pressure, from the center out. (If the dough seems very sticky at first, add flour liberally; but if it becomes sticky only after you roll it for a few minutes, return it to the refrigerator for 10 minutes before proceeding.) Continue to roll, adding small amounts of flour as necessary, rotating the dough occasionally, and turning it over once or twice during the process. (Use ragged edges of dough to repair any tears, adding a drop of water while you press the patch into place.) When the dough is about 10 inches in diameter (it will be less than ¼ inch thick), place your pie plate upside down over it to check the size.

5   Move the dough into the pie plate by draping it over the rolling pin or by folding it into quarters, then moving it into the plate and unfolding it. When the dough is in the plate, press it firmly into the bottom,

sides, and junction of bottom and sides. Trim the excess dough to about ½ inch all around, then tuck it under itself around the edge of the plate. Decorate the edges with a fork or your fingers, using any of the methods illustrated at right. Freeze for 10 minutes (or refrigerate for 30 minutes).

6 When you're ready to bake, prick it all over with a fork.

Ⓜ **Generous Pie Shell for a 10-Inch or Larger Pie, or a Deep-Dish Pie** Increase flour to 1½ cups, salt to ¾ teaspoon, sugar to 1½ teaspoons, butter to 10 tablespoons, water to 4 tablespoons.

Ⓜ **Pie Shell for a Two-Crust Pie** Increase flour to 2¼ cups, salt to 1 teaspoon, sugar to 2 teaspoons, butter to 16 tablespoons, water to 6 tablespoons. Proceed with directions in Step 1 and 2 of Flaky Pie Crust, forming the dough into a ball. Cut the dough in half, shape it into two balls, and wrap them in plastic. Flatten each into a disk and chill. Roll and transfer each crust as described beginning in Step 3.

Ⓜ Prebaked Flaky Pie Crust

For any single-crust pie, 8 to 10 inches in diameter • Time: About 30 minutes

It's important to prebake—or "blind bake"—pie crusts for which the filling would burn if the filled pie were baked the full time needed for the crust to become crisp and brown. This applies to custard pies, which loosely includes Pecan Pie (page 90) and Pumpkin Pie (page 91).

1 recipe Flaky Pie Crust (at left), or frozen and pricked all over with a fork at ½-inch intervals   **Unsalted butter as needed**

1 Preheat the oven to 425°F. Tear off a piece of foil large enough to fit over the entire crust when folded in half; fold it. Smear butter on one side of the foil, then press it into the crust. Weight the foil with a pile of dried beans or rice (these can be reused for this same purpose), pie weights, or a tight-fitting skillet or saucepan—anything that will sit flat on the surface.

2 Bake 12 minutes. Remove from the oven, reduce the heat to 350°F, and carefully remove the weight and foil.

3 Bake another 10 to 15 minutes, or until the crust is a beautiful shade of brown. Remove and cool on a rack.

Fluting a Pie Crust

You can flute the edges of a pie crust in a variety of different ways. Three of the easiest are:

Pinch the dough between the side of your forefinger and your thumb.

Press a knuckle from one side into the space made by your thumb and forefinger on the other.

Simply press down with the tines of a fork along the edges of the dough.

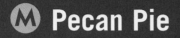 Pecan Pie

There are two types of pecan pies, one of which contains not only sugar but also corn syrup. I don't like this version—not only is it too sweet, if you taste corn syrup by itself you'll never cook with it again. The other thickens the sugar with eggs—in other words, it's a custard pie, loaded with pecans. What could be better than that? Toast the pecans first for best flavor.

Makes about 8 servings

Time: About 1½ hours

1 Flaky Pie Crust (page 88)

2 cups shelled pecans

5 eggs

1 cup white sugar

½ cup brown sugar

Pinch salt

6 tablespoons (¾ stick) butter, melted

1 tablespoon vanilla extract

1 Prepare pie crust dough. Follow Steps 1 and 2 of Prebaked Flaky Pie Crust (page 89) to begin baking. While the crust is in the oven, toast the pecans and start the filling. When the crust is done, turn the oven to 425°F.

2 Place the pecans on a baking sheet and bake (you can do this before the oven reaches 425°F), shaking and stirring, for about 5 minutes, or until the pecans are hot. Cool the pecans; coarsely chop half of them and leave the other half intact. Lower the oven to 375°F.

3 For the filling: Beat the eggs well, until they are foamy. Beat in the sugars, salt, and butter. While the crust is baking, warm this mixture in a medium saucepan over medium-low heat, stirring occasionally, until it is hot to the touch; do not boil. Stir in the vanilla extract and the pecans.

4 Place the pie plate on a baking sheet. Pour this mixture into the still-hot crust and bake 30 to 40 minutes, until the mixture shakes like Jell-O but is still quite moist. Cool on a rack and serve warm or at room temperature.

Chocolate Pecan Pie Steps 1 and 2 remain the same. Before beginning Step 3, melt 2 ounces semisweet chocolate with 3 tablespoons of butter until smooth. Let cool while you beat the eggs, sugars, and salt (omit the remaining butter). Combine the chocolate and egg mixtures and warm gently as in Step 3, then proceed as above.

Pumpkin Pie

A tradition of such long standing that it's almost impossible not to serve one; fortunately, the preparation is quite simple. Feel free to adjust the spices to your taste. Some people don't like cloves, so omit them. Many people like much more cinnamon—you can taste before you bake, and add more.

Makes about 8 servings

Time: About 1½ hours

1 Flaky Pie Crust (page 88)

3 eggs

¾ cup sugar

½ teaspoon ground cinnamon

⅛ teaspoon freshly grated nutmeg

½ teaspoon ground ginger

Pinch ground cloves

Pinch salt

2 cups canned or fresh pumpkin puree or cooked

2 cups half-and-half, light cream, or whole milk

1   Prepare pie crust dough. Follow Steps 1 and 2 of Prebaked Flaky Pie Crust (page 89) to begin baking. While the crust is in the oven, start the filling. When the crust is done, turn the oven to 375°F.

2   For the filling: Beat the eggs with the sugar, then add the spices and salt. Stir in the pumpkin puree and then the half-and-half. Warm this mixture in a medium saucepan over medium-low heat, stirring occasionally, until it is hot to the touch; do not boil.

3   Pour the mixture into the still-hot crust and bake 30 to 40 minutes, until the mixture shakes like Jell-O but is still quite moist. Cool on a rack and serve warm or at room temperature.

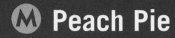 Peach Pie

This is the classic two-crusted peach pie—a delight for summer events. Substitute an equal weight of other similar stone fruit, such as nectarines, plums, or apricots, if you like. Please: Use perfectly ripe fruit if at all possible.

Makes about 8 servings

Time: About 1½ hours

About 2 pounds peaches, or a little more (6 to 10 peaches, depending on their size)

1 tablespoon freshly squeezed lemon juice

About ½ cup sugar, more if the peaches are not quite ripe, plus a little for the top of the pie

¼ teaspoon ground cinnamon or ½ teaspoon almond extract

⅛ teaspoon freshly grated nutmeg or ground allspice, if you use cinnamon

1½ tablespoons cornstarch or 2 tablespoons instant tapioca

1 recipe Pie Shell for a Two-Crust Pie (page 89), bottom crust fitted into a 9-inch pie pan, top crust transferred to a rimless baking sheet, both refrigerated

2 tablespoons unsalted butter, cut into bits

Milk as needed

1 Peel the peaches: Bring a pot of water to the boil and drop the peaches into it, a couple at a time, for 10 to 30 seconds, or until the skins loosen. Plunge into a bowl of ice water. Slip the peels off, using a paring knife to ease the process. Pit, slice, and toss with the lemon juice.

2 Mix together the dry ingredients (including the almond extract, if you're using it), and toss the peaches with this mixture. Pile into the rolled-out shell, making the pile a little higher in the center than at the sides. Dot with butter. Carefully transfer the top crust from the baking sheet to the pie plate, covering the filling and pressing the edges together with those of the bottom crust to form a seal. Trim if necessary, and decorate the edges with a fork or your fingers, using any of the methods illustrated on page 89. Refrigerate while you preheat the oven to 450°F.

3 Place the pie on a baking sheet and brush the top lightly with milk; sprinkle with sugar. Use a sharp paring knife to cut two or three 2-inch-long vent holes in the top crust; this will allow steam to escape.

4 Place in the oven and bake for 10 minutes. Reduce the heat to 350°F and bake another 40 to 50 minutes, or until the pie is golden brown. Do not underbake. Cool on a rack before serving warm or at room temperature.

Ⓜ Peach-and-Berry Pie Add 1 cup berries (blueberries are best) to the mixture of peaches or other fruit.

Ⓜ Cherry Pie Sour cherries are best for pie. Substitute 4 to 5 cups pitted sour cherries for the peaches; omit the lemon juice unless you're using sweet cherries. Proceed as above. If you use canned cherries, drain them well and increase the thickener by 1 tablespoon.

Classic Chocolate Chip Cookies

For parties, gift giving, or any time, even the most basic chocolate chip cookie from this main recipe is irresistible. Double or triple the recipe, add ingredients as in the variation, and you have a collection of special and well-appreciated cookies. This recipe makes a typically chewy chocolate chip cookie, one with a little height. Add 2 tablespoons milk or water to the batter if you want a flatter, crisper cookie.

Makes 3 to 4 dozen

Time: About 30 minutes

½ pound (2 sticks) unsalted butter, softened

¾ cup white sugar

¾ cup brown sugar

2 eggs

2 cups (9 ounces) all-purpose flour

½ teaspoon baking soda

½ teaspoon salt

1 teaspoon vanilla extract

2 cups chocolate chips

1 Preheat the oven to 375°F.

2 Use an electric mixer to cream together the butter and sugars; add the eggs one at a time and beat until well blended.

3 Combine the flour, baking soda, and salt in a bowl and add them to the batter by hand, stirring to blend. Stir in the vanilla and then the chocolate chips. Drop by teaspoons or tablespoons onto ungreased baking sheets and bake until lightly browned, about 10 minutes. Cool for about 2 minutes on the sheets before using a spatula to transfer the cookies to a rack to finish cooling. Store in a covered container at room temperature for no more than a day or two.

Ⓜ Chunky Cookies In place of (or in addition to) the chocolate chips, use M&Ms (or other similar candy), or roughly chopped walnuts, pecans, or cashews; slivered almonds; raisins; coconut; dried cherries; and so on. Or combine any chunky ingredients you like.

Butter Drop Cookies

Handle this batter gently; good butter cookies are tender, and overworking the batter will develop the gluten in the flour and make them tough.

Makes 2 to 3 dozen

Time: About 30 minutes

2 cups (9 ounces) all-purpose flour

½ teaspoon baking powder

Pinch salt

8 tablespoons (1 stick) unsalted butter, softened if combining by hand or mixer, chilled if using a food processor, plus some for greasing the baking sheets

¾ cup sugar

1 teaspoon vanilla extract

1 egg

¼ cup milk, plus more if needed

1 Preheat the oven to 375°F.

2 To combine the ingredients by hand, mix the flour, baking powder, and salt together in a small bowl. Cream the butter with a fork, then mash in the sugar until well blended. Stir in the vanilla and the egg, then about half the flour mixture. Add the milk, then the remaining flour, then a little more milk, if necessary, to make a soft batter that can be dropped from a spoon.

To combine the ingredients with an electric mixer, combine the flour, baking powder, and salt together in a small bowl. Place the butter and sugar in the mixing bowl and beat on low speed until well blended and creamy. Add the vanilla and the egg and beat on low speed until well combined. Add about half the flour mixture, beat for a moment, and then add the milk. Beat for about 10 seconds, then add the remaining flour and a little more milk, if necessary, to make a soft batter that can be dropped from a spoon.

To combine the ingredients in a food processor, place all the dry ingredients in the processor and pulse once or twice to combine. Cut the chilled butter into bits, add to the machine, and process for about 10 seconds, until butter and flour are well blended. Add the vanilla, egg, and milk and pulse just enough to blend. If more milk is needed to make a soft batter than can be dropped from a spoon, add it by hand.

3 Drop rounded teaspoons of the batter onto buttered baking sheets and bake for about 10 minutes, or until the edges are browned. Let each sheet sit on a rack for 2 minutes before removing the cookies with a spatula and cooling them on a rack. Store in a covered container at room temperature for no more than a day or two.

Preparation Tips: When you cream butter for cookies or cakes, use an electric mixer (or a fork), and the butter is much easier to work if it is slightly softened. If you plan ahead by an hour or so, this presents no problems. If, however, you decide to make cookies or a cake on the spur of the moment, you will want to soften the butter more quickly.

To soften butter quickly, cut the butter into small cubes (say, 16 cubes for a stick of butter, easily accomplished), or microwave on the lowest power for 10-second intervals, removing the butter well before it actually begins to melt.

Baking Tips: Drop cookies can (and should) be made as the oven is preheating. They are soft, buttery, sweet, and, because they have height, perfect for containing other ingredients. (The chocolate chip is the paradigm of drop cookies.)

To adjust any drop cookie recipe to your taste, remember this: Butter makes cookies tender, flour makes them cakey, shorter cooking times (within reason, of course) produce chewier cookies, and longer ones make them crispier.

Ⓜ Chocolate Drop Cookies A combination of unsweetened and sweetened chocolate is good here, but you can use all sweetened if you prefer (if you use all unsweetened, increase the sugar to 1 cup). Increase the milk very slightly, to about 1/3 cup. Melt 1 ounce each semisweet and unsweetened chocolate and add to the mixture after combining wet and dry ingredients.

Ⓜ Sour Cream or Sugar Drop Cookies The use of sour cream not only gives you a tangy taste but also lets you use baking soda, whose flavor is less obtrusive than that of baking powder. And these may be dropped, or refrigerated for about 1 hour, then rolled into walnut-sized balls before baking. Substitute 1 teaspoon baking soda for the all of the baking powder. Substitute sour cream for the milk; you will need about 1/2 cup. To make sugar cookies, roll the dough balls in sugar, or sprinkle drop cookies with sugar halfway through baking.

5 Simple Ideas for Butter Cookies

1 To make butter nut cookies, add 1/2 cup chopped nuts to the finished batter.

2 To make butterscotch cookies, use 2/3 cup brown sugar in place of the white sugar.

3 To make orange or lemon cookies, add 1 tablespoon grated or minced orange or lemon zest to the finished batter; omit the vanilla. Add 2 tablespoons poppy seeds as well, if you like.

4 To make raisin cookies, add up to 1/2 cup raisins or chopped dried fruit to the finished batter.

5 To make cinnamon cookies, dust the cookies with a mixture of 2 tablespoons white sugar and 1 teaspoon ground cinnamon just before baking.

Refrigerator (Rolled) Cookies

Refrigerator cookies—also called rolled cookies, because they can be rolled out and cut with a lightly floured cookie cutter (or that old standby, a glass)—must be made in advance. This can be an advantage, because you can make the dough days ahead and bake them whenever you get the urge (it's a disadvantage when you don't have the dough but you want cookies, like right now). You can also freeze the dough, and need not defrost it before baking, as long as you're happy to slice it instead of rolling and cutting it into shapes.

These are ideal for cookie-cutter cookies because refrigerating a stiff cookie dough makes it easy to roll out. That doesn't mean you must do so; the alternative is to shape the dough into logs and slice it thinly before baking. Generally, rolled

Makes at least 3 dozen

Time: 30 minutes, plus time to chill

½ pound (2 sticks) unsalted butter, softened, plus some for greasing the baking sheets

1 cup sugar

1 egg

3 cups (about 14 ounces) all-purpose flour, plus some for dusting the work surface

Pinch salt

1 teaspoon baking powder

1 tablespoon milk

1 teaspoon vanilla extract

1 Use an electric mixer to cream the butter and sugar together until light; beat in the egg.

2 Combine the flour, salt, and baking powder in a bowl. Mix the dry ingredients into the butter-sugar mixture, adding a little milk at a time as necessary. Stir in the vanilla.

3 Shape the dough into a disk (for rolled cookies) or a log (for sliced cookies), and refrigerate for at least 2 hours, or as long as 2 days (or wrap very well, and freeze indefinitely).

4 Preheat the oven to 400°F. Cut the dough disk in half. Lightly flour a work surface and a rolling pin and roll gently until about ⅛ inch thick, adding flour as necessary and turning the dough to prevent sticking. Cut with any cookie cutter. (To slice, simply cut slices from the log, about ⅛ inch thick.)

5 Bake on lightly greased baking sheets until the edges are lightly browned and the center set, 6 to 10 minutes. Let rest on the sheets for a minute or two before removing with a spatula and cooling on a rack. Store in a covered container at room temperature for no more than a day or two.

cookies are more crumbly and less chewy than drop cookies. But if you want them on the chewy side, underbake them just a little bit, removing them from the oven while the center is still a little soft.

I like the flavor and texture of cookies that are very dense and rich in butter—not unlike shortbread—but there are alternatives; see below.

To glaze cookies, drizzle or spread them with a mixture of 1 cup confectioners' sugar and just enough milk or cream to make a thin paste—about 1/3 cup. Or decorate before baking with sprinkles or other tiny candies.

Preparation Tip: If you're not eating or serving cookies right away, it's better to freeze the finished batter rather than to freeze baked cookies—especially refrigerator cookies—wrap the log in a couple of layers of plastic and freeze. You can then slice directly from the freezer (30 minutes of thawing will make that job a little easier) and bake.

Baking Tip: Most ovens have hot spots, and it usually doesn't matter much. But with cookies, it can make a difference, so, halfway through the estimated baking time, turn the baking sheets back to front; if you're cooking more than one sheet at the same time, rotate them top to bottom as well.

Ⓜ Fancier Rolled Cookies After rolling and cutting (or slicing), top each cookie with a pecan, walnut, or other nut; a raisin or other piece of dried fruit; an M&M or other small candy; some sprinkles; or any other decoration you like. Or glaze the baked and cooled cookies with chocolate: Melt 8 ounces semisweet chocolate with 3 tablespoons unsalted butter. Spread mixture onto one side of the cookies, then lay on cooling rack until chocolate coating is firm.

Ⓜ Peanut Butter Cookies In Step 1, cream 1/2 to 3/4 cup peanut butter with the butter-sugar mixture. You can use smooth or crunchy peanut butter, as you like. You can also add about 1/2 cup chopped peanuts (try those with salt for an interesting change), along with the vanilla, in Step 2.

5 Simple Ideas for Rolled Cookies

1 Add 1 cup dried unsweetened coconut to the butter-sugar mixture, alternating with the flour.

2 Add 1 cup chopped walnuts, pecans, almonds, or hazelnuts to the batter along with the vanilla. Or add 1/2 cup nuts and 1/2 cup raisins.

3 Add 1 teaspoon ground ginger to the flour mixture; for a super-ginger flavor, add 1/4 cup minced crystallized ginger to the butter-sugar mixture.

4 Dust cookies with mixture of 2 tablespoons white sugar and 1 teaspoon ground cinnamon just before baking.

5 Replace vanilla extract with 1/2 teaspoon almond extract. Use in combination with chopped nuts if you like.

Ⓜ Aunt Big's Gingersnaps

These are super-crisp gingersnaps, the kind that stick in your teeth, and are savory enough to eat in place of dinner. "The dough is also great undercooked," says my friend Sally, who is Aunt Big's niece. For gingerbread people, see the variation.

Makes 4 to 5 dozen

Time: About 40 minutes, plus time to chill

½ pound (2 sticks) unsalted butter, softened

1 cup sugar

1 cup molasses

1 heaping teaspoon baking soda

2 tablespoons hot water

3½ cups (about 1 pound) all-purpose flour

1 heaping tablespoon ground ginger

1 tablespoon ground cinnamon

Pinch salt

1 Use an electric mixer to cream the butter, sugar, and molasses until smooth. Mix the baking soda with 2 tablespoons hot water and beat into this mixture.

2 Mix together the flour, spices, and salt in a bowl; stir them into the butter mixture and beat well. Shape into 2 long rolls, wrap in waxed paper, and refrigerate several hours or overnight.

3 Preheat the oven to 350°F. Slice the cookies as thinly as you can, place on ungreased baking sheets, and bake about 10 minutes, watching carefully to prevent burning. Remove from sheet when still warm and cool on a rack. Store in a covered container at room temperature for several days.

Ⓜ **Gingerbread Men** Remove the refrigerated dough from the refrigerator about 15 minutes before beginning to work; preheat the oven. When the dough is slightly softened, roll it out as thinly as possible; hand-cut if you're brave, or use a gingerbread man cutter. Bake as above, then cool. Decorate, if you like, with small candies and a glaze made from confectioners' sugar thinned with milk. Store in a covered container at room temperature for up to several days.

Ⓜ **Molasses-Spice Cookies** Add ½ teaspoon freshly grated nutmeg, ⅛ teaspoon ground cloves, and ¼ teaspoon ground allspice along with the ginger.

This is simpler than a pie and delicious—made with an almond crust and the best berry jam you can find.

Makes about 8 servings

Time: About 1½ hours

1 cup blanched almonds

1½ cups all-purpose flour

Pinch salt

½ cup sugar

¼ teaspoon ground cinnamon

Pinch ground cloves

12 tablespoons (1½ sticks) cold butter, cut into pieces

1 teaspoon grated or minced lemon zest

2 egg yolks

1 teaspoon ice water if needed

About 1½ cups quality raspberry jam

Freshly squeezed lemon juice (optional)

Confectioners' sugar for dusting

1 Preheat the oven to 400°F. Place the almonds on a baking sheet and bake for 5 to 10 minutes. Turn the oven to 425°F. Cool the almonds, then place them in the container of a food processor and grind them finely. Add the remaining dry ingredients and pulse to blend. Add the butter and lemon zest and process until the mixture is crumbly, about 10 seconds.

2 Remove the dough from the food processor and use a wooden spoon or a rubber spatula to blend in the egg yolks; gradually gather the mixture into a ball. (If the mixture is too dry, add 1 teaspoon ice water.) Wrap the ball in plastic or waxed paper, flatten into a small disk, and freeze the dough for 10 minutes (or refrigerate for 30 minutes).

3 Roll out about two-thirds of the dough, keeping the remainder wrapped in plastic. Place the dough in an 8- or 9-inch tart pan. Prick the crust all over with a fork. Bake 12 minutes, or just until it begins to darken. Remove and cool on a rack; turn the oven to 350°F.

4 Taste the jam; if it is too sweet, cut it with a little lemon juice. When the shell is cool, spread on the jam. Make a lattice (below) with the reserved dough, and place it on top of the jam. Bake for about 40 minutes, or until the crust is brown and the jam is very hot. Remove and sprinkle with a little confectioners' sugar. Cool on a rack, and serve at room temperature.

Making a Lattice Top

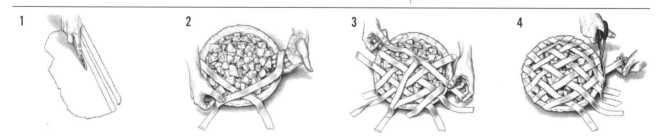

(Step 1) Roll out a piece of dough a couple of inches longer than the pie plate, and 5 or 6 inches wide. Cut ten ½-inch strips. (Step 2) Weave the strips over the top of the pie. (Step 3) Continue to weave, bending back the strips laid in one direction in order to add strips in the other. (Step 4) When done weaving, press edges into the crust and trim.

Death-by-Chocolate Torte

This chocolate layer cake with cream filling and a rich chocolate glaze is the kind of thing that restaurants would have you believe is magic. On the contrary, there are only two challenges here: assembling the ingredients, and clearing out enough time.

Makes at least 10 servings

Time: About 3 hours, largely unattended

---

8 tablespoons (1 stick) unsalted butter, softened, plus some for greasing the pan and the paper

1 cup (about 4½ ounces) all-purpose flour, plus some for dusting the pan

3 ounces unsweetened chocolate

½ cup water

7 eggs

1 cup plus 2 tablespoons sugar

2 teaspoons vanilla extract

Pinch salt

2 tablespoons unsweetened cocoa powder

1 Preheat the oven to 350°F. Butter the bottom and sides of a 9-inch layer cake pan; cover the bottom with a circle of waxed or parchment paper, butter the paper, and sift a little flour over the whole pan; invert to remove the excess flour.

2 Melt the 3 ounces of chocolate with the water over low heat; cool. Use an electric mixer to beat 5 of the eggs until light; gradually add 1 cup of the sugar, continuing to beat until the mixture is very thick. Gently stir in half the flour, then the chocolate mixture, then the remaining flour, and finally half of the vanilla and a pinch of salt. Turn into the prepared cake pan and bake 40 to 50 minutes, until the cake is firm and a toothpick inserted in the center comes out dry, or nearly so. Cool for 5 minutes before turning out onto a rack.

3 To make the butter cream, place 2 egg yolks (reserve the whites for another use, or discard) in the container of a blender. Add the remaining sugar, remaining vanilla, and the cocoa. Turn on the blender and add the butter, a little bit at a time. When the butter is blended in, chill to a spreading consistency.

4 When the cake is completely cool, use a serrated knife to carefully split it in half horizontally. Spread the bottom layer with chilled butter cream, then put the top layer in place. Chill for an hour or so, then make Dark Chocolate Glaze, below. Use a lightly oiled spatula to spread the glaze over the top and sides of the torte. Serve small slices, with whipped cream (see Tip), if you like. Because of its dense texture, this cake keeps better than most; you can cover and refrigerate it for up to a couple of days—it will remain a treat.

Preparation Tip: To make fresh whipped cream, start with very cold heavy cream or whipping cream. (Whip it straight from the refrigerator.) Using a whisk, eggbeater, or mixer, whip the cream until it barely holds a soft peak. Sweeten the cream about halfway through whipping. You can make it ahead and store it, covered, in the refrigerator for several hours. If it separates, beat it a little to blend.

Dark Chocolate Glaze

Makes enough to cover 1 (9-inch) layer cake • Time: 10 minutes

If you fill your cake with jam or butter cream (as in the Death-by-Chocolate Torte at left), and you love dark chocolate, this is the perfect finish for your cake. It's bittersweet and rich, very intense, but you don't use that much; it isn't a filling, just a glaze. Apply it while it's hot, with an oiled spatula, on a chilled cake; it will solidify perfectly and almost instantly.

¾ cup top-quality unsweetened cocoa powder

½ cup heavy cream

6 tablespoons (¾ stick) unsalted butter, cut into bits

¾ cup confectioners' sugar

Tiny pinch salt

½ teaspoon vanilla extract

1 Mix together the cocoa, cream, butter, confectioners' sugar, and salt in a small saucepan. Cook over low heat until combined and thickened, 5 to 10 minutes.

2 Stir in the vanilla and use immediately.

8 | Desserts and Drinks

 Make Ahead

This simple, no-egg rice pudding is sweet and easy. See the list (below) for ways to make it special.

Makes 8 servings

Time: 40 minutes

2 cups water

1 cup long- or short-grain rice

Dash salt

2 cups milk

¾ cup sugar, or more to taste

1 teaspoon ground cinnamon or cardamom

1 Bring the water to a boil in a medium saucepan; stir in the rice and the salt. Cover and cook over low heat until almost all the water is absorbed, about 20 minutes.

2 Uncover, pour in the milk and cook, stirring frequently, until about half the milk is absorbed. Stir in the sugar and spice and continue to cook until the rice is very soft and the milk absorbed. About halfway through cooking, taste and add more sugar if necessary.

3 Spoon into custard cups and serve warm or cold, garnished with whipped cream (page 101) if you like. This keeps well for 2 days or more, covered and refrigerated.

5 Simple Ideas for Rice Pudding

1 Add ¼ cup or more raisins, or snipped dates, figs, or other dried fruit about halfway through the cooking.

2 Use canned coconut milk, in place of some or all of the milk.

3 Add 1 teaspoon of vanilla extract or orange blossom or rose water at the end of cooking.

4 Add 1 teaspoon minced lemon or orange zest in place of the spice.

5 Garnish with a sprinkling of toasted sliced almonds or other nuts.

# Lemon Mousse

A refreshing cold mousse, wonderful for spring and summer festivities or any time you want a rich, rewarding end to the meal. It contains cream and eggs but is stabilized by gelatin, which makes it virtually foolproof. Use any citrus you like in place of the lemon. Raw eggs carry some danger of salmonella, a risk of which you are probably aware. But undercooked eggs (like fried eggs with runny yolks) are equally "dangerous." I have made this mousse many times with only positive results, but cook the way that makes you comfortable.

Makes at least 6 servings

Time: About 30 minutes, plus time to chill

---

1 (¼ ounce) package unflavored gelatin

½ cup freshly squeezed lemon juice

4 eggs

1 tablespoon grated or minced lemon zest

½ cup sugar

1 cup heavy cream

Whipped cream, mint or lemon verbena leaves, berries, or toasted almonds for garnish

1 In a small saucepan, sprinkle the gelatin over the lemon juice and let sit while you proceed to Step 2.

2 Beat the eggs, lemon zest, and sugar with a whisk or electric mixer until lemon-colored and slightly thickened.

3 Warm the gelatin mixture over low heat, stirring occasionally, until the gelatin dissolves, just a minute or two. Cool for 1 minute, then stir into the egg mixture.

4 Working quickly (you don't want the gelatin to set up prematurely), whip the cream until it holds soft peaks, then stir thoroughly into the egg mixture.

5 Refrigerate, stirring occasionally for the first hour or two, until well chilled. Garnish and serve the same day.

# Peanut Brittle

If you've never made peanut brittle, you will not believe how simple it is—or how quickly it disappears. It makes a great gift, too—it's easy to store, ships well, and stays fresh.

Makes about 1 pound

Time: About 20 minutes, plus time to cool

Unsalted butter for greasing the pan

2 cups sugar

2 cups roasted peanuts, salted or unsalted, your choice

Pinch salt if you're using unsalted peanuts

1 Use the butter to grease a baking sheet, preferably one with a low rim.

2 Place the sugar in a large, heavy skillet and turn the heat to low. Cook, stirring occasionally, until the sugar turns liquid. Then stir constantly until it turns golden but not brown.

3 Stir in the peanuts and the salt if you're using it and immediately pour the mixture onto the greased baking sheet. Cool, then break into pieces. (If you like, you can score the brittle with a knife when it has solidified slightly but not yet turned hard; that way, it will break into even squares.) Store in a covered container for as long as you like.

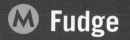 **Fudge**

Like so many things, the best fudge is made with good, common ingredients. Here, the two that matter most are top quality chocolate and fresh cream, preferably not ultra-pasteurized. This requires some patience, but results in a winning party dessert, holiday gift, or special treat anytime.

Makes about 1½ pounds

Time: About 30 minutes, plus resting time

2 tablespoons unsalted butter, plus some for greasing the pan

4 ounces unsweetened chocolate, chopped

1 cup heavy cream

2 cups sugar

Pinch salt

1 teaspoon vanilla extract

½ to 1 cup chopped (not minced) walnuts or pecans (optional)

1 Let the butter come to room temperature while you work; grease a 9-inch square baking pan.

2 Combine the chocolate and cream in a medium saucepan over low heat. Cook, stirring constantly, until well blended and smooth. Add the sugar and salt, still over low heat, and cook, stirring, until the mixture boils.

3 Stop stirring and cook until the mixture measures 236°F or "soft ball" candy stage (a small piece of it will form a soft ball when dropped into a glass of cold water, but the thermometer is an easier and surer test).

4 Immediately remove from the heat. Add the butter, but do not beat. When the mixture is just lukewarm, add the vanilla and beat vigorously with a wooden spoon until the mixture is smooth and has lost its sheen. Add the nuts if you like. Scrape into the prepared pan. When the mixture has hardened, cut into squares. Wrap well and refrigerate; fudge keeps for weeks, but is best eaten fresh.

Chocolate Truffles

An irresistible gift or meal finale. If you like your chocolate sweet, add the optional sugar here, but these truffles are plenty sweet without it. They're also best eaten the same day they're made.

Makes about 2 dozen

Time: About 2 hours, largely unattended

8 ounces semisweet or bittersweet chocolate

2 tablespoons water

2 tablespoons unsalted butter

¾ cup heavy cream

2 tablespoons confectioners' sugar (optional)

Unsweetened cocoa powder

1 In a small saucepan over low heat, melt the chocolate with the water, stirring occasionally, until smooth, then add the butter a bit at a time, stirring to blend after each addition.

2 Gradually add the cream, stirring after each addition until the mixture is smooth. Taste and stir in some or all of the confectioners' sugar if you like. Refrigerate until cool and stiff, about an hour.

3 Sift some cocoa powder onto a plate (alternatively, you can grind ½ cup toasted skinned almonds in a blender or spice mill with ¼ cup confectioners' sugar and use that). Line another plate with waxed paper. Use two spoons or your hands to make small balls out of the chocolate mixture, and roll them in the powder. Place on the waxed paper and serve immediately, or refrigerate for up to a day or two.

Shopping Tip: Time after time, Valrhona chocolate—made in France—wins taste testings of fine chocolates. And, though it may not be the best chocolate in the world, it is probably the best that you can find in most metropolitan areas. Though not the most expensive chocolate, it is pricey, but its presence will make simple truffles like these much better. Of course, if you're going to that effort and expense, you'd better make sure you have good butter and cream as well.

4 Additional Truffle Coatings

1 Grated coconut, or toasted grated coconut

2 Finely chopped nuts, such as almond or pistachio

3 Colored sprinkles

4 Finely chopped chocolate or white chocolate

Hot Chocolate

To make hot chocolate for one, use 8 ounces milk, 1½ tablespoons cocoa, and 2 tablespoons sugar, or to taste. A tiny bit of vanilla extract, added at the last moment, is a welcome addition here; or you may prefer a little mint.

Makes 4 servings

Time: 10 minutes

---

4 cups whole, reduced-fat, or skim milk

¼ cup powdered cocoa, such as Hershey's (or use 2 squares of unsweetened baking chocolate, chopped)

¼ cup sugar, or to taste

Pinch salt

1 Pour the milk into a blender, then add the other ingredients, and turn the machine on; let run for 10 seconds or so. Alternatively, blend the dry ingredients with about ½ cup of the milk over very low heat in a small saucepan, stirring until smooth. Stir in the rest of the milk, beating with a fork or wire whisk.

2 Heat the mixture over medium-low heat (or in a microwave), stirring occasionally, until hot. Pour into cups and serve.

Mocha Hot Chocolate Substitute freshly brewed coffee for half or more of the milk.

Mulled Wine or Cider

Do not boil the wine; just warm it gently. If you're making this for a party, keep it warm in a coffee urn or similar warming container.

Makes 4 to 6 servings

Time: 15 minutes

---

1 bottle (750 milliliters) dry red wine or cider

1 lemon, sliced

1 orange, sliced, plus several orange slices reserved for garnish

1/4 teaspoon freshly grated nutmeg, or to taste

2 cloves

1 (3-inch) piece cinnamon stick or 1/2 teaspoon ground cinnamon

Sugar to taste (optional)

1 Combine the first six ingredients in a medium saucepan; turn the heat to medium-low. Cook, stirring occasionally, until quite hot to the touch but not boiling. Add sugar if needed and stir to dissolve.

2 Strain out the solids and serve, garnished with fresh orange slices.

Hot Buttered Rum

The grown-up equivalent of hot cocoa—perfect when you're chilled to the bone. Add a pinch of ground cloves, cinnamon, and/or nutmeg if you like.

Makes 1 serving

Time: 5 minutes

---

1 cup water

1 teaspoon butter

1 teaspoon sugar, or to taste

3 tablespoons (1½ ounces) rum

1 Bring water to a boil.

2 Place the remaining ingredients in a mug and pour boiling water over them. Stir and serve.

Shopping Tip: When buying rum, as is the case with so many liquors, the most popular brands are also the worst. Look for a dark rum from Puerto Rico—it's likely to be inexpensive, too—and use that. The flavor will be superior to that of any pale light or clear rum.

Ⓜ Egg Nog

Real egg nog is a super-treat, with or without rum.

Makes 4 servings

Time: 10 minutes

---

3 eggs, separated

2 tablespoons sugar, or to taste

½ teaspoon vanilla extract

3 cups milk or half-and-half

½ cup rum (optional), or more if desired

Freshly grated nutmeg to taste

1 Beat the egg yolks with the sugar until well blended. Stir in the vanilla, the milk or half-and-half, and rum if desired.

2 Beat the egg whites and fold them in thoroughly. (You need not be too gentle; they should lighten the drink but not be discernible.) Top with grated nutmeg and serve.

Holiday Menus

M Dishes That Can Be Made Ahead

Breads, Pies, Cookies, Cakes

Desserts and Drinks

Tips Reference

Here's an at-a-glance reference of the tips in this book. If you're ever looking for some quick info—on cookies, for example—you can look here, instead of scanning the index and flipping through recipe pages trying to find it. The page reference leads you back to the related recipe, if you want to consult it.

Apples   You can make your own applesauce by cooking a few pounds of apples, cut in half (if you have a food mill, you need not peel and core them, but otherwise you must), with about 1/2-inch of water in a covered pot. Turn the heat to medium-high. When the mixture bubbles, uncover and turn it to low. Cook, stirring occasionally, until the apples break down, about 30 minutes. Let cool, then add sugar if necessary. Put through the food mill, discarding the solids that remain. *See page 71.*

Bacon   Both slab bacon and smoked ham hocks are sold in most supermarkets (those without additives are best). *See page 78.*

Blue cheese   Blue cheese can be made from the milk of goats, cows, or sheep. Goat blue has the distinctive flavor associated with all goat cheeses, and tends to be less creamy than the other two. The best known blue sheep cheese is Roquefort. Usually, however, it's easier to find a good Gorgonzola or Stilton (both made from cow's milk), or a good domestic variety, like Maytag blue. Good blue cheese should be quite soft, though not runny. *See page 16.*

Bouillabaisse   Anise liqueur—Pernod and Ricard are the most common brands—is a strong-flavored drink from France, related to ouzo (Greece), raki (Turkey), and a handful of other such spirits. The flavor is traditional in bouillabaisse, and also makes a great drink, over ice, with a splash of water or soda. *See page 25.*

Bread crumbs   To make bread crumbs, break fairly fresh or quite stale bread into chunks, and grind in a food processor or blender, a few chunks at a time. Toast crumbs on a baking sheet for 10 minutes in a 350°F oven if you like, or store untoasted and toast, if you like, before using. Store bread crumbs in a sealed plastic bag in the freezer; they will keep forever. *See page 37.*

Brussels sprouts   With Brussels sprouts, the smaller the better is a good rule. Reject any with yellow leaves, loose leaves, or those that are soft or not tightly packed. Generally, they are a winter vegetable, found from September or October through early spring. *See page 67.*

Remove the Brussels sprouts stem and any loose leaves. Some people suggest cutting an "x" in the root bottom to ensure even cooking, but I haven't found that it matters much. *See page 67.*

Butter   To soften butter quickly, cut the butter into small cubes (say, 16 cubes for a stick of butter, easily accomplished), or microwave on the lowest power for 10-second intervals, removing the butter well before it actually begins to melt. *See page 95.*

Chestnuts   In much of Europe, chestnuts fall to the ground through September and October, so the best season is definitely autumn. Buy heavy, big, full, unblemished nuts; they dry out as they age, and begin to rattle around in their shells. Their shelf life is not as long as you might think—just a week or two; refrigeration is neither necessary nor helpful. *See page 69.*

Cooked, shelled, and skinned chestnuts are good mashed with butter, just like potatoes, or braised with other vegetables or meats, or gently sautéed. *See page 69.*

Chocolate   Time after time, Valrhona chocolate—made in France—wins taste testings of fine chocolates. And, though it may not be the best chocolate in the world, it is probably the best that you can find in most metropolitan areas. Though not the most expensive chocolate, it is pricey, but its presence will make simple truffles like these much better. Of course, if you're going to that effort and expense, you'd better make sure you have good butter and cream as well. *See page 108.*

Clams   Clams and mussels should be alive when you buy them. This will mean that hard-shell clams (littlenecks, cherrystones, quahogs, etc.) will have closed, undamaged shells that will be next to impossible to open with your hand. Mussels and soft-shell clams (steamers) will have gaping, undamaged shells that will move when you click them together. *See page 25.*

Buying clams is easy, because those in the shell must be alive. When hard-shells die, you can move their shell apart; otherwise, they're shut up pretty tight, and you cannot even slide their shells from side to side. Live soft-shells (steamers) react visibly to your touch, retracting their necks and closing slightly (they are never closed all the way—hence the name "gapers"). Dead clams smell pretty bad, so it's unlikely you'll be fooled. *See page 35.*

Store clams in a bowl in the refrigerator, where they will remain alive for several days. *See page 35.*

Hard-shell clams—like littleneck quahogs and cherrystones—require little more than a cleaning of their shells. I use a stiff brush to scrub them under running water. To shuck them, see the illustrated steps on page 24. Small hard-shells—under two inches across—are nice lightly steamed, like mussels, or stuffed and baked. *See page 35.*

Cookies   When you cream butter for cookies or cakes, use an electric mixer (or a fork), and the butter is much easier to work if it is slightly softened. If you plan ahead by an hour or so, this presents no problems. If, however, you decide to make cookies or a cake on the spur of the moment, you will want to soften the butter more quickly. *See page 95.*

Drop cookies can (and should) be made as the oven is preheating. They are soft, buttery, sweet, and, because they have height, perfect for containing other ingredients. (The chocolate chip is the paradigm of drop cookies.) *See page 95.*

To adjust any drop cookie recipe to your taste, remember this: Butter makes cookies tender, flour makes them cakey, shorter cooking times (within reason, of course) produce chewier cookies, and longer ones make them crispier. *See page 95.*

If you're not eating or serving cookies right away, it's better to freeze the finished batter rather than to freeze baked cookies—especially refrigerator cookies—wrap the log in a couple of layers of plastic and freeze. You can then slice directly from the freezer (30 minutes of thawing will make that job a little easier) and bake. *See page 97.*

Most ovens have hot spots, and it usually doesn't matter much. But with cookies, it can make a difference, so, halfway through the estimated baking time, turn the baking sheets back to front; if you're cooking more than one sheet at the same time, rotate them top to bottom as well. *See page 97.*

Crab	Most crabmeat is from the familiar 4- to 6-inch blue crab or—on the West Coast—rock or Dungeness crab. Often sold whole and live, crab is also cooked, its meat picked from the shell wherever it grows, to be sold throughout the country, refrigerated or frozen. When sold as picked meat, "lump" means large pieces from the body, "flake" means smaller pieces, but "claw" is best. Fresh crabmeat is expensive, but incredibly convenient and wonderfully flavorful; even with a squirt of lemon, it's celestial. *See page 34.*
Cranberries	Cranberries should be firm and whole; you can freeze them almost indefinitely, or store them in the refrigerator for weeks. Incredibly, it doesn't make much difference. *See page 75.*
Duck confit	If you can find duck confit (preserved duck)—it's sold in some specialty markets—it makes a super addition here. Crisp it up in a skillet and add it at the last minute, or simmer it along with the rest of the meat. A piece of duck breast, seared just before serving, also makes the cassoulet more special. *See page 63.*
Goat cheese	Mesclun is a good place for fresh goat cheese, something that is made locally in many communities throughout the country. But a slightly aged, camembert-like goat cheese is good here, too. *See page 14.*
Goose	Goose is nearly always sold frozen; you order it in advance then thaw it yourself. The easiest way to thaw goose is to let it sit in the refrigerator for 2 days before you plan to cook it. If you're in a hurry, defrost it by letting it sit in cold water, changing the water occasionally; but you should still plan for it to take the better part of a day for a 10-pound bird. *See page 49.*
Green beans	You can choose any of a number of green beans: the thin haricot vert (common in France), the yard-long bean (originally from China, now grown here also), the wax or yellow bean (obviously not green at all), and the romano, a gardening favorite. All can be eaten raw, briefly cooked—so that they remain crunchy—or cooked to complete tenderness. *See page 70.*
	Sold year-round, green beans are at their best in summer, when they're most likely to be local. Buy beans that snap rather than fold when you bend them in half, and avoid any with browning or other obvious signs of spoilage. *See page 70.*
	Store green beans, loosely wrapped in plastic, in the vegetable bin, and use as soon as possible, preferably within a day. *See page 70.*
Grilling	If you plan to use wooden skewers for grilling, soak them first in cold water for at least 30 minutes, to prevent them from burning during the cooking. *See page 11.*
Ham	Most supermarket hams, including canned hams, are just a step above the heavily processed ham you buy at the deli counter. For good-quality ham, mail order is usually your best bet; find a brand you like and stick to it. A good old-fashioned cure begins with a real brine of salt, water, and sugar, and concludes with a long period of smoking. A high-tech cure begins with a chemically augmented injected brine and ends with a douse of liquid smoke. You can taste the difference. *See page 58.*
Lamb	If you find or create a larger boneless leg—sometimes they are up to 6 pounds—either cut off a piece and freeze it for later use, or make the whole thing, but increase the other ingredients proportionally and plan to serve 8 to 12 people. *See page 61.*

When buying rack of lamb, make sure it's not too large (2 pounds is the maximum) and ask the butcher to make sure the chine bone (backbone) is removed. This will allow you to easily cut through the ribs to separate them at the table. *See page 62.*

Don't bother to ask to have the lamb ribs "frenched" (the meat removed from the top of the bones); the crisp meat along the bones is one of the pleasures of a rack of lamb. *See page 62.*

Latkes   For different latkes, you can substitute grated sweet potatoes (or, for that matter, carrots) for about one-third of the white potatoes—no more, or the mixture will not be sufficiently starchy. *See page 71.*

Lobster   When you're buying lobster, lift each one (make sure its claws are pegged or banded); if it doesn't flip its tail and kick its legs, look for another. *See page 36.*

Two people sharing a 3-pound lobster will get more meat of equally high quality than if each eats a 1½-pound lobster. There's less work, less waste, and more meat hidden in those out-of-the-way places. *See page 36.*

Mozzarella   In recent years, fresh mozzarella has begun to appear in more and more markets. Packed in water and sold in bulk, it is creamier, more tender, and more flavorful than the standard mozzarella sold dry and wrapped in plastic. Store it at home in its water and use it as quickly as possible, preferably within a day or two. *See page 8.*

Octopus   Most octopus is cleaned and frozen at sea; defrost it in the refrigerator, or in cold water. *See page 19.*

Many will tell you to tenderize octopus before cooking. I don't. I cook it until it is tender, which can take time but is simpler than some of the "tenderizing" methods. *See page 19.*

Oysters   Oyster names are confusing, because they more often refer to where they're grown or harvested than what type they are: The Atlantic variety—also called Eastern—is almost always called by its place names, like Bluepoint, Wellfleet, and Apalachicola; the European oyster (the one most aficionados prefer)—also known as the "flat" (plat in French)—is sometimes called Belon, a name that belongs to a small region in France; the Pacific oyster, grown all over the world, is sometimes called a Portuguese ("Portugaise"), from a now-extinct species that once made up the majority of oysters grown in Europe. *See page 39.*

If you're cooking oysters, the differences are less important. Use those that have been shucked, packaged, and marked with a "sell-by" date. But for oysters on the half-shell, you first have to determine which oyster you like (see above), and then make sure the shells are undamaged and shut tight. *See page 39.*

To clean oysters, just scrub the shells thoroughly with a not-too-stiff brush. There's never any sand inside. *See page 39.*

Shucking oysters is the truly difficult part; see illustrations (page 38), but also ask your fishmonger if he can do it for you. Keep them on a bed of crushed ice and eat them within a couple of hours. *See page 39.*

Pears   Though some people like pears as hard as apples, most prefer them soft, though not completely mealy. They're at their best when their "shoulders"—the part where they taper—yield readily to a firm touch. *See page 16.*

Potatoes   Baking potatoes (Idaho or Russet) are best for potato pancakes, because they're high in starch, so they will bind better. All-purpose potatoes like Yukon Gold do a decent job as well. If you're stuck with low-starch potatoes ("new," whether red or white), add an extra egg and a little more bread crumbs. *See page 71.*

Pumpkin   Unless you want a jack-o'-lantern, buy small pumpkins—3 pounds is big enough. Avoid those with soft spots. Store at room temperature or refrigerate for up to a month. *See page 23.*

Use a cleaver or very large knife to split the pumpkin in half or cut wedges. Scoop out the seeds and strings and discard. To peel, use a paring knife, and don't fret if you take a fair amount of the flesh with the skin; it's unavoidable. *See page 23.*

Quiche   The doughs for quiches are best made with butter, but can also be made with olive oil. The flavor will be excellent, the texture not so great, but if you are off butter, you'll probably think the trade-off worthwhile. *See page 10.*

Bear in mind that quiches have savory crusts, and so can be flavored in any way you like: Add 1 teaspoon of minced Roasted Garlic (page 5) to the crust, or 1 teaspoon to 1 tablespoon of any herb that you're using in the filling, for example. Cornmeal substituted for about one-quarter of the flour also makes for a nice change, adding crunch and flavor. *See page 10.*

Like any custard, quiche filling should be cooked gently so it becomes creamy rather than hard. For this reason, and to keep the crusts crisp, crusts are precooked at high temperature, then filled and returned to the oven at lower temperature. *See page 10.*

Roast   If you want the best roast, make a special request for the small end (the 12th through the 7th ribs) and ask the butcher—even a supermarket butcher can do this—to cut it to order for you, removing the short ribs; you want what's called a "short" roast. *See page 53.*

If you are serving prime rib roast to 4 to 6 people, buy 3 or 4 ribs (higher numbers are better, so look for ribs 12 through 10, or 9); if you're serving more, add another rib for every 2 people, unless you want to serve gargantuan portions. I usually buy a 3-rib roast for up to 6 people and have leftovers, but I believe in serving lots of side dishes when I make a roast so no one is tempted to eat a pound of meat. *See page 53.*

For rare meat, figure about 15 to 20 minutes per pound roasting for any prime rib roast, regardless of the size, but see the recipe for details. All beef is rare at 125°F (120°F for really rare); there are noticeable differences in meat color for each 5° difference in temperature. I'd never cook anything beyond 155°F, although some cooks suggest cooking roast beef to 170°F for well done. Large roasts will rise at least 5° in temperature between the time you remove them from the oven and the time you carve them. *See page 53.*

Cutting into a piece of meat to check its doneness is far from a sin; it's one of those things that everyone does but no one talks about. So if you're at all in doubt, cut into the middle of the roast or take a slice from the end. Your presentation will not be as beautiful but if the meat is perfectly cooked no one will care. *See page 53.*

Rum   When buying rum, as is the case with so many liquors, the most popular brands are also the worst. Look for a dark rum from Puerto Rico—it's likely to be inexpensive, too—and use that. The flavor will be superior to that of any pale light or clear rum. *See page 111.*

Salmon   The cooking time for salmon varies according to your taste. I prefer my salmon cooked to what might be called medium-rare to medium, with a well-cooked exterior and a fairly red center. So, I always look at the center of a piece of salmon to judge its doneness. Remember that fish retains enough heat to continue cooking after it has been removed from the heat source, so stop cooking just before the salmon reaches the point you'd consider it done. *See page 29.*

Farm-raised salmon (it's usually Atlantic salmon) is available year-round and is fairly flavorful and usually inexpensive. Wild salmon, from the Pacific Northwest, is only available fresh from spring to fall, but it's preferable, especially if you can find king (chinook), sockeye (red), or coho (silver). Chum and pink salmon are less valued but still good wild varieties. *See page 29.*

Few supermarkets will scale salmon fillets for you, so the easiest thing to so is to cook the fish with the scales on and simply peel off the skin (which takes almost no effort once the fish is cooked). This works well, because the scales give added protection against overcooking, and come right off with the skin. *See page 29.*

Buying a whole salmon, once a challenge, has become a snap thanks to the presence of (almost) always-fresh farm-raised salmon. Call your fishmonger or supermarket a day ahead, because they may have to order one (most salmon is shipped already filleted); but they should have no trouble getting it. *See page 30.*

Seafood   Seafood salad works well as part of a feast; you can vary the ingredients as you like, including more raw vegetables, and a larger or smaller variety of fish, depending on what is available. For example, if you don't have sardines, you can skip them entirely. *See page 19.*

Shrimp   Because almost all shrimp is frozen before sale, it makes some sense to buy still-frozen shrimp rather than those that have been thawed. Because the shelf life of previously frozen shrimp is not much more than a couple of days, buying thawed shrimp gives you neither the flavor of fresh nor the flexibility of frozen. Stored in the home freezer, shrimp retain their quality for a month or more. *See page 32.*

Learn to judge shrimp size by the number it takes to make a pound, as retailers do. Shrimp labeled "16/20," for example, require 16 to 20 individual specimens to make a pound. Those labeled "U-20" require fewer (under 20) to make a pound. Shrimp of from 15 or 20 to about 30 per pound usually give the best combination of flavor, ease (peeling tiny shrimp is a nuisance), and value. *See page 32.*

Shrimp should be peeled if it's to be cooked in a sauce that will make it difficult to peel them at the table. They might also be peeled if you're feeling generous or energetic. The shells, by the way, make a super broth. For simple grilling or pan-cooking, however, it's arguable that shrimp with their peels on lose less liquid and flavor. *See page 32.*

Shrimp is among the easiest shellfish to cook. It isn't always done when it turns pink—some larger shrimp take a little longer to cook through—but it usually is. Cut one open to be sure. *See page 32.*

Some people won't eat shrimp that isn't deveined (others believe that the "vein," which is actually the animal's intestinal tract, contributes to flavor). I can neither detect the presence of the vein when it is left in nor notice its absence when it is removed, so I ignore it. Devein if you like. *See page 33.*

Spinach   Fresh spinach leaves must be plump; any wilting or yellowing is a bad sign. Store it, loosely wrapped in plastic, in the vegetable bin, but use it as fast as you can. It will keep for a few days. Sold year-round, in season locally in cool but not cold or hot weather. Wash it well, in several changes of water; it's sandy. Remove the thickest stems, but leave thinner ones on; they'll be fine. *See page 74.*

Squash   Peel butternut squash with a paring knife; its skin is too tough for a vegetable peeler (and be ruthless, rather than careful; squash is cheap). The densest, best "meat" is in the narrow part, where there are no seeds, so use that part first. *See page 68.*

Squid   Frozen squid, typically cleaned before freezing, is available in supermarkets for less that $2 a pound. Fresh squid should be purple to white, not brown. The smell should be clean and sweet, and the skin should shine. *See page 19.*

Stuffing   If you want a moist, soft, juicy stuffing, pack it in the bird. But if you want a clean-flavored, crisp stuffing that can stand on its own as a side dish, consider cooking it on its own. (And, although this is not really a concern if you cook your birds thoroughly —the temperature of the stuffing needs to reach 165°F, just like the meat—the chances of harmful bacteria developing in the bird are greater if you cook the stuffing inside of it.) *See page 80.*

Don't skimp on the fat or the seasonings. Lean, underseasoned stuffing is little more than mushy bread. *See page 80.*

Sweet potatoes   Sweet potatoes are the familiar bright orange-fleshed tubers (more exotic varieties have rose, purple, yellow, or white flesh) of fall and winter. They are not yams, which—popular nomenclature to the contrary—are a different tuber. *See page 73.*

Brilliant baked, sweet potatoes are also good handled in many of the same ways you would treat white potatoes and winter squash—fried, mashed, or roasted. *See page 73.*

Turkey   You can easily make stock with leftover turkey. Roast the meat and bones along with a few carrots or onions until browned. Then add water and simmer for about an hour. Cool, strain, and season with salt and pepper. *See page 21.*

Whipped cream   To make fresh whipped cream, start with very cold heavy cream or whipping cream. (Whip it straight from the refrigerator.) Using a whisk, eggbeater, or mixer, whip the cream until it barely holds a soft peak. Sweeten the cream about halfway through whipping. You can make it ahead and store it, covered, in the refrigerator for several hours. If it separates, beat it a little to blend. *See page 101.*

Wild rice   If you can, avoid the little boxes of wild rice you find in the supermarket; the price is outrageous, and the quality suspect. Look for a good mail order source (you might start with www.zingermans.com). *See page 77.*

Index

Conversions, Substitutions, and Helpful Hints

Cooking at High Altitudes

Every increase in elevation brings a decrease in air pressure, which results in a lower boiling point. At 7,000 feet, for example—the altitude of many towns in the Southwest—water boils at 199°F. This means slower cooking times (and makes a pressure cooker a more desirable appliance). Families who have been living in the mountains for years have already discovered, though trial and error, the best ways to adjust.

Newcomers to high altitudes must be patient and experiment to discover what works best. But here are some general rules for high-altitude cooking:

1. For stove-top cooking, use higher heat when practical; extend cooking times as necessary. Beans and grains will require significantly more time than at sea level.

2. Assume that batters and doughs will rise faster than at sea level.

3. Over 3,000 feet, increase baking temperatures by 25°.

4. Over 3,000 feet, reduce baking powder (or other leavening) measurements by about 10 percent; increase liquid in baked goods by the same percentage. You may want to reduce the amount of sugar slightly as well.

5. For every 2,000-foot increase in altitude above 3,000 feet, reduce leavening even further.

Imperial Measurements

Theoretically, both the United Kingdom and Canada use the metric system, but older recipes rely on the "imperial" measurement system, which differs from standard U.S. measurements in its liquid ("fluid") measurements:

$\frac{1}{4}$ cup = 2.5 ounces

$\frac{1}{2}$ cup ("gill") = 5 ounces

1 cup = 10 ounces

1 pint = 20 ounces

1 quart = 40 ounces

Some Useful Substitutions

1 cup cake flour = $\frac{7}{8}$ cup all-purpose flour + $\frac{1}{8}$ cup cornstarch

1 tablespoon baking powder = 2 teaspoons baking soda + 1 teaspoon cream of tartar

1 cup buttermilk = 1 scant cup milk at room temperature + 1 tablespoon white vinegar

1 cup brown sugar = 1 cup white sugar + 2 tablespoons molasses

1 cup sour cream = 1 cup yogurt (preferably full fat)

Measurement Conversions

Note that volume (i.e., cup) measures and weight (i.e., ounce) measures convert perfectly for liquids only. Solids are a different story; 1 cup of flour weighs only 4 or 5 ounces.

Dash or pinch = less than $\frac{1}{4}$ teaspoon

3 teaspoons = 1 tablespoon

2 tablespoons = 1 fluid ounce

4 tablespoons = $\frac{1}{4}$ cup = 2 fluid ounces

16 tablespoons = 1 cup = 8 fluid ounces

2 cups = 1 pint

2 pints = 1 quart

4 quarts = 1 gallon

Imperial vs. Metric

These are approximate, but are fine for all uses.

1 ounce = 28 grams

1 pound = 500 grams or $\frac{1}{2}$ kilo

2.2 pounds = 1 kilo

1 teaspoon = 5 milliliters (ml)

1 tablespoon = 15 milliliters

1 cup = $\frac{1}{4}$ liter

1 quart = 1 liter

Doneness Temperatures

Use an instant-read thermometer for the best possible accuracy; always measure with the probe in the thickest part of the meat, not touching any bone (ideally, measure in more than one place). When you gain experience in cooking, you'll be able to judge doneness by look and feel.

Beef

125°F = Rare

130–135°F = Medium-rare

135–140°F = Medium

140–150°F = Medium-well

155°F + = Well-done

Pork

137°F = Temperature at which trichinosis is killed

150°F = Slightly pink but moist

160°F = Well-done (and probably dry)

Chicken

160°F = Breast is done

165°F = Thigh is done

Lamb

125°F = Very rare

130°F = Rare

135°F = Medium-rare

140°F = Medium

150°F = Medium-well

160°F + = Well-done

USDA—Recommended Internal Temperatures

The recommended internal temperatures given in this book for meats and poultry are based on producing the best-tasting food, and are in line with traditional levels of doneness. The United States Department of Agriculture (USDA), however, generally recommends higher temperatures, which reduces the potential danger of contracting illness caused by bacteria.

Beef, Veal, and Lamb

Ground meat (hamburger, etc.) 160°F

Roasts, Steaks, and Chops

145°F = Medium-rare

160°F = Medium

170°F = Well-done

Pork (all cuts including ground)

160°F = Medium

170°F = Well-done

Poultry

Ground chicken and turkey: 165°F

Whole chicken and turkey: 180°F

Stuffing: 165°F

Poultry Breasts: 170°F

Poultry Thighs: Cook until juices run clear

Egg Dishes: 160°F